Quick Study

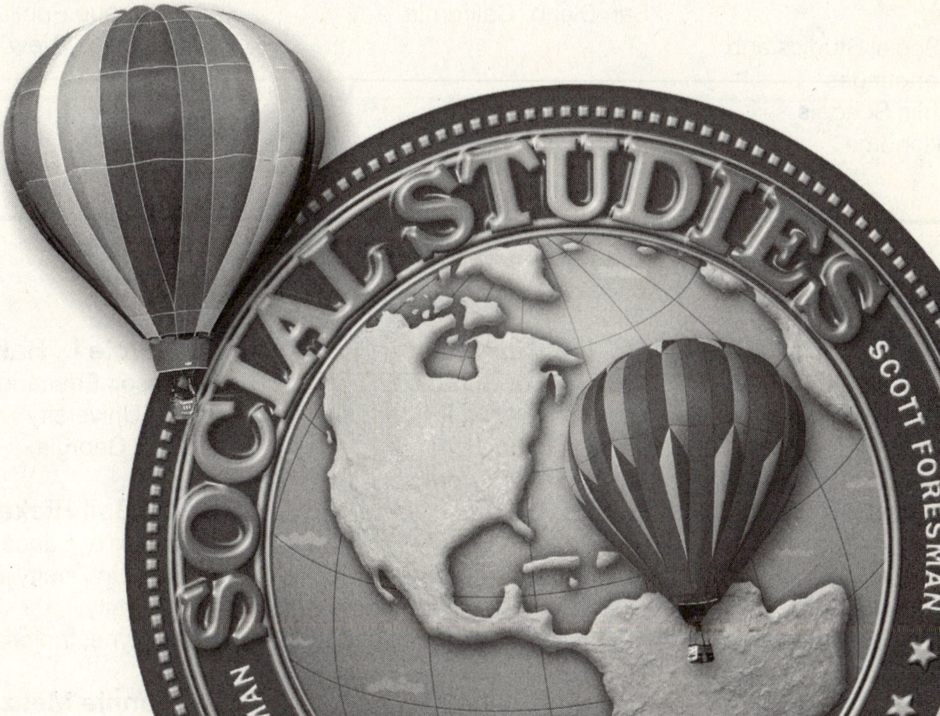

PEARSON
Scott Foresman

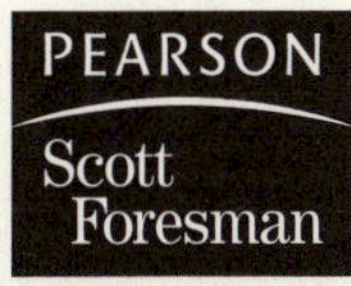

Editorial Offices: Glenview, Illinois • Parsippany, New Jersey • New York, New York
Sales Offices: Parsippany, New Jersey • Duluth, Georgia • Glenview, Illinois • Coppell, Texas • Ontario, California • Mesa, Arizona

www.sfsocialstudies.com

Program Authors

Dr. Candy Dawson Boyd
Professor, School of Education
Director of Reading Programs
St. Mary's College
Moraga, California

Dr. Geneva Gay
Professor of Education
University of Washington
Seattle, Washington

Rita Geiger
Director of Social Studies and Foreign Languages
Norman Public Schools
Norman, Oklahoma

Dr. James B. Kracht
Associate Dean for Undergraduate Programs and Teacher Education
College of Education
Texas A&M University
College Station, Texas

Dr. Valerie Ooka Pang
Professor of Teacher Education
San Diego State University
San Diego, California

Dr. C. Frederick Risinger
Director, Professional Development and Social Studies Education
Indiana University
Bloomington, Indiana

Sara Miranda Sanchez
Elementary and Early Childhood Curriculum Coordinator
Albuquerque Public Schools
Albuquerque, New Mexico

Contributing Authors

Dr. Carol Berkin
Professor of History
Baruch College and the Graduate Center
The City University of New York
New York, New York

Lee A. Chase
Staff Development Specialist
Chesterfield County Public Schools
Chesterfield County, Virginia

Dr. Jim Cummins
Professor of Curriculum
Ontario Institute for Studies in Education
University of Toronto
Toronto, Canada

Dr. Allen D. Glenn
Professor and Dean Emeritus
Curriculum and Instruction
College of Education
University of Washington
Seattle, Washington

Dr. Carole L. Hahn
Professor, Educational Studies
Emory University
Atlanta, Georgia

Dr. M. Gail Hickey
Professor of Education
Indiana University-Purdue University
Fort Wayne, Indiana

Dr. Bonnie Meszaros
Associate Director
Center for Economic Education and Entrepreneurship
University of Delaware
Newark, Delaware

ISBN 0-328-09004-2

10-V016-12 11 10 09 08 07

Contents

Name ____________________ Date ____________ **Lesson 1 Summary**

Use with pages 10–15.

Lesson 1: Communities

Vocabulary

community a place where people live, work, and have fun together

geography the study of Earth and how people live on it

Carlos's Community

Carlos lives in the community of El Paso, Texas. A **community** is a place where people live, work, and play together. Carlos thinks his community is special for many reasons. The **geography,** or land around his community, is different from others. El Paso lies in a pass between two sets of mountains. It is also next to Mexico, the country south of the United States.

What Is a Community?

In a community, people work together and care about one another. There are rules to follow in a community. These rules keep everyone safe. Many people have jobs in their community. They work as teachers, letter carriers, police officers, doctors, and grocery store workers or in many other jobs. All of these things are important to a community.

History of El Paso

El Paso has a very long history. It is over 400 years old! Native Americans first lived in El Paso. Later the Spanish came. There are still many old buildings from those early days. Some special celebrations in El Paso come from Spanish history. Nearby, there is a river called the Rio Grande. Across the river is a different community that people can visit. This community is Juarez, Mexico.

Life in El Paso

El Paso is a city. It is part of the state of Texas. Texas is part of the country of the United States of America. The United States of America is a country on the continent of North America. North America is part of the planet Earth. Families are important parts of their communities. Families of El Paso do things that families of other communities do. Some of these things are working, voting, and helping others.

Name ______________________ Date ____________ **Lesson 1 Review**

Use with pages 10–15.

Lesson 1: Review

1. **Main Idea and Details** Fill in the main idea in the diagram below.

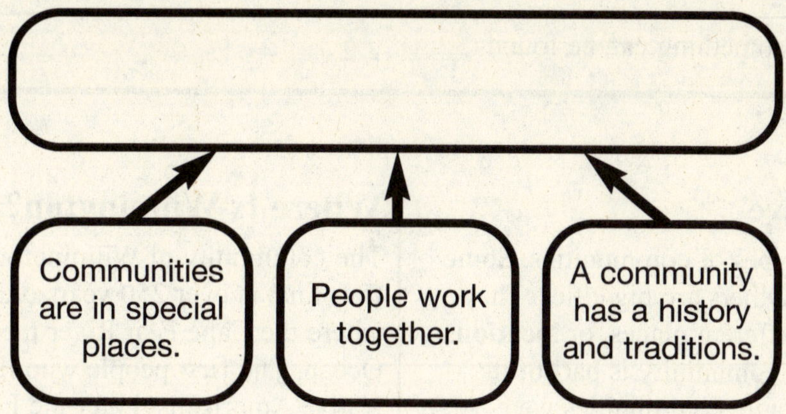

2. Tell about the geography of El Paso.

____

____

____

3. Tell about the history of El Paso.

____

____

____

4. Name the state and country where El Paso is located.

____

____

____

5. **Critical Thinking: *Draw Conclusions*** Why do you think people came to live in El Paso?

____

____

____

Use with pages 18–23.

Lesson 2: United States Communities

Vocabulary

location where something can be found

Where We Live

There are many types of communities. Some are small towns. Others are big cities. They are found in all different places, or **locations.** The location of a community is part of its geography. Long ago, communities were located near lakes, rivers, or oceans. People had not built good roads yet. Instead, people used boats to move people and goods. Also, farms were built on land good for growing things.

Where Is Astoria?

Astoria, Oregon, is located where the Columbia River meets the Pacific Ocean. The community of Astoria is almost 200 years old. Many people in Astoria have parents or grandparents from a part of Europe called Scandinavia. Many people in Astoria like to boat, swim, and fish. They also like to ride waves in the Pacific Ocean. Astoria has many museums to visit.

Where Is Wilmington?

The community of Wilmington, North Carolina, is over 250 years old. It is located where the Cape Fear River meets the Atlantic Ocean. The first people who lived there were Native Americans. Later the English came. There are interesting things to see and do in Wilmington. Airlie Gardens has birds and flowers. Many people swim in the ocean. Others explore Fort Fisher. Fort Fisher is a sand fort.

Where Is Denver?

Denver, Colorado, is located at the foot of the Rocky Mountains. The community of Denver is near the middle of the United States. It is located where Cherry Creek meets the South Platte River. Many people like to walk in the mountains. Native Americans were the first people to live in this area. They were called the Arapaho. Later, gold was found in Denver. More people moved there to look for gold.

Use with pages 18–23.

Lesson 2: Review

1. **Main Idea and Details** Fill in the main idea that tells about these communities.

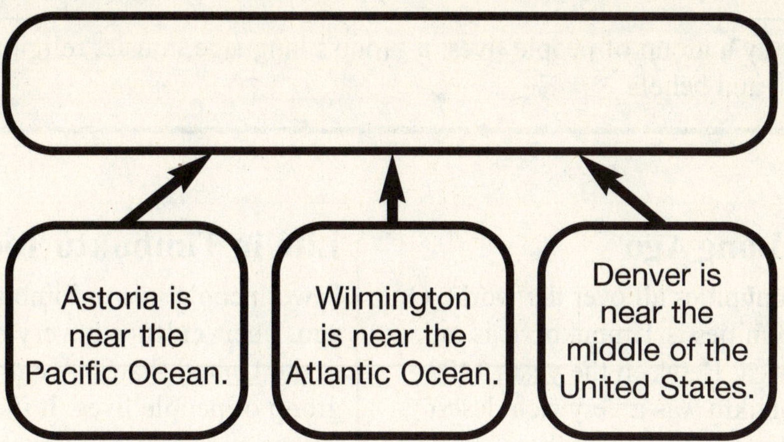

2. Why were the early communities often located near rivers or oceans?

____

____

____

3. Tell about the geography of the communities of Astoria, Wilmington, and Denver.

____

____

____

4. Tell about the first settlers in Astoria, Wilmington, and Denver.

____

____

____

5. **Critical Thinking: *Compare and Contrast*** Compare and contrast the fun things people do in the communities of Astoria, Oregon; Wilmington, North Carolina; and Denver, Colorado.

____

____

____

Name ______________________ Date ____________ **Lesson 3 Summary**

Use with pages 26–29.

Lesson 3: World Communities

Vocabulary

culture the way a group of people lives; a group's language, music, religion, food, clothing, holidays, and beliefs

Timbuktu Long Ago

There are communities all over the world. One of these communities is Timbuktu. It is in Mali, West Africa. Between the years 1400 and 1600, Timbuktu was a very rich desert city. Thousands of people lived there. Traders brought salt and other goods to Timbuktu. They traded the salt for gold. Religion was very important in Timbuktu. In the 1500s, there was a huge university in the city. Many people went there to go to school.

Life in Timbuktu Today

Fewer people live in Timbuktu today than long ago. Their **culture** is very different from ours in the United States. A culture is the way a group of people lives. It includes a group's language, music, religion, food, clothing, holidays, and beliefs. Many people in Mali speak the languages of Bambara and French. Their homes are made of mud bricks. There are few good roads in Mali. People travel by walking, taking buses, or riding camels. The weather in Timbuktu is hot and dry. Religion is still very important there.

Name ______________________ Date ____________

Use with pages 26–29.

Lesson 3: Review

1. **Main Idea and Details** Fill in some details about the culture of Timbuktu.

The culture of Timbuktu is made of many parts.

The people speak French and Bambara.

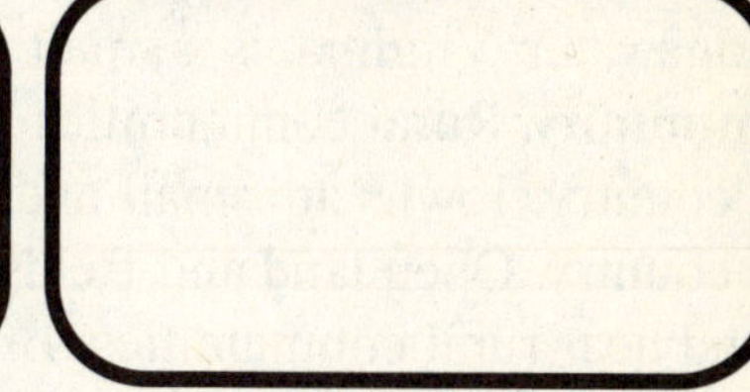

2. Tell about what makes up the culture of a community.

____

____

____

3. How is the community of Timbuktu today different from the way it was between 1400 and 1600? How is it the same?

____

____

____

4. When was Timbuktu a very wealthy city?

____

____

____

5. **Critical Thinking: *Compare and Contrast*** How is the community of Timbuktu today like your community? How is it different?

____

____

____

Name ______________________ Date ____________

Use with pages 38–41.

Lesson 1: A Rural Community

Vocabulary

rural community a community located in the country

Amy's Rural Community

Bridgewater, Virginia, is a small **rural community.** Rural communities are located in the country. Towns are small and far apart in the country. Open land and fields are usually found near rural communities. Bridgewater is in the state of Virginia. It is in the Shenandoah Valley. Bridgewater is in Rockingham County. It sits on the North River. About 5,000 people live in Bridgewater. A lot of its people work in larger communities that are near Bridgewater.

Community Life

Bridgewater is small, but there is a lot to do there. People meet to talk about farming and the community. They belong to the 4-H Club. Children play sports such as baseball. They also join scouting groups. Many people like living in Bridgewater. Almost everyone in town knows and helps one another.

Name ______________________ Date ____________ **Lesson 1 Review**

Use with pages 38–41.

Lesson 1: Review

1. **Main Idea and Details** Fill in some of the details that tell about life in a rural community.

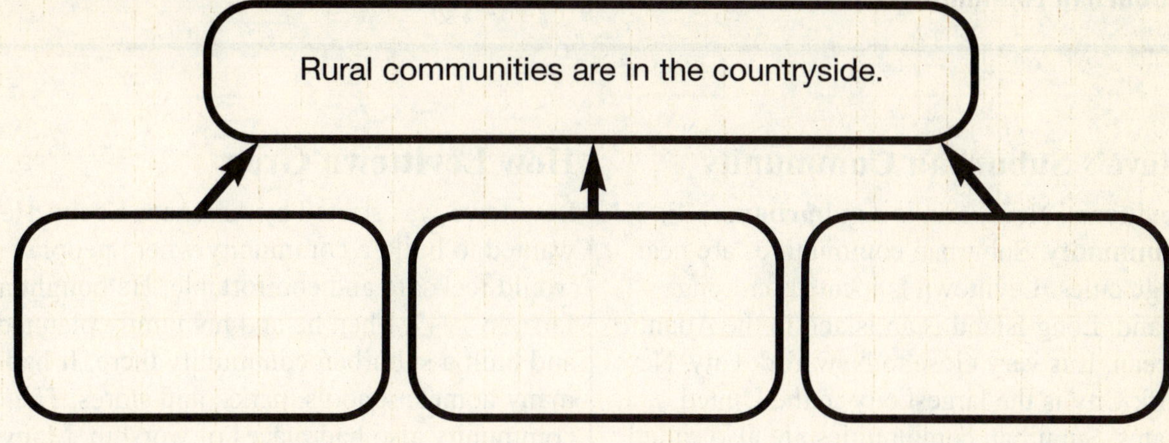

2. What is a rural community?

____

____

____

3. Describe the different ways that people in Bridgewater have fun.

____

____

____

4. Describe the location of Bridgewater.

____

____

____

5. **Critical Thinking: *Observe*** How do you think that Bridgewater might have gotten its name?

____

____

____

Name ______________________ Date ____________ **Lesson 2 Summary**

Use with pages 42–45.

Lesson 2: A Suburban Community

Vocabulary

suburban community a community near a large city

Steve's Suburban Community

Levittown, New York, is a **suburban community.** Suburban communities are near large cities. Levittown is located on Long Island. Long Island is an island in the Atlantic Ocean. It is very close to New York City. New York City is the largest city in the United States. Suburban communities are also called suburbs. Many people who live in suburbs such as Levittown work in the large city nearby. People in Levittown have fun at parks and beaches.

How Levittown Grew

Levittown was started by Abraham Levitt. He wanted to build a community where people would feel safe and comfortable. He bought a farm in 1947. Then he and his family planned and built a suburban community there. It had many homes, schools, parks, and stores. The community also had places of worship. Many people moved there from New York City. Other suburban communities were built in the United States. Highways helped suburbs grow. They let people get to work easily.

Name ____________________ Date __________ **Lesson 2 Review**

Use with pages 42–45.

Lesson 2: Review

1. **Main Idea and Details** Fill in the main idea about suburban communities.

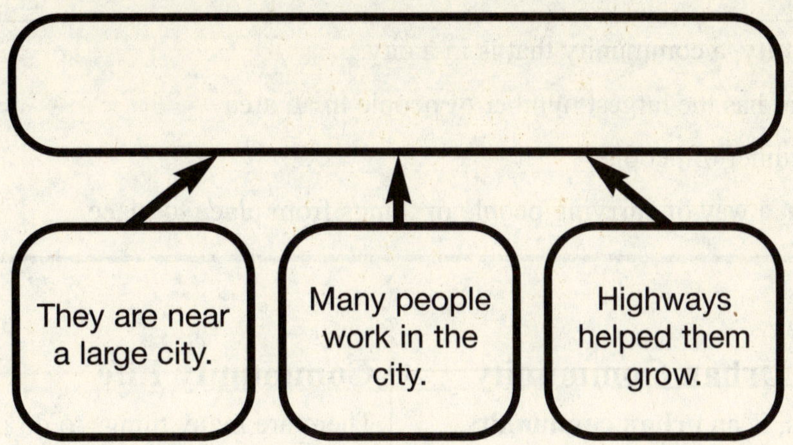

2. What steps did Levitt take to change a farm into a suburb?

____

____

____

3. What did Levitt include in his community plan?

____

____

____

4. What are some needs that lead people to form communities?

____

____

____

5. **Critical Thinking: *Observe*** Tell how transportation is important to your community.

____

____

____

Name ____________________ Date __________ **Lesson 3 Summary**

Use with pages 48–53.

Lesson 3: An Urban Community

Vocabulary

urban community a community that is in a city

city a place that has the largest number of people in an area

population number of people

transportation a way of carrying people or things from place to place

Chicago, an Urban Community

Chicago, Illinois, is an **urban community.** An urban community is located in a **city.** Urban communities have large **populations.** The population of Chicago is more than three million people. Chicago is in the midwestern part of the United States. It is on the western shore of Lake Michigan. A fur trader moved to the area in 1779. Later, a town grew there. The town was first called Chicago in 1837.

Working in Chicago

In Chicago, people work in many different places. They work in department stores, banks, and offices. They also work in the Sears Tower, the tallest office building in the United States. **Transportation** helps people move around the city. Transportation is important because so many people need to get to work. Many people ride on buses or the "El" train. The "El" is a raised train that runs through the city.

Community Life

There are many things to do in Chicago. In the summer, people watch the boats on Lake Michigan. They also go to the beach or have picnics. Many people like to watch plays at the theaters in Chicago. Chicago also has many museums. Many people visit the Art Institute. The Adler Planetarium is in Chicago. Many people go there to learn about outer space. People visit the city's aquarium to learn about sea life. They also go to see the water coming out of Buckingham Fountain.

Name _______________ Date _______

Lesson 3 Review

Use with pages 48–53.

Lesson 3: Review

1. **Main Idea and Details** Fill in some details about life in an urban community.

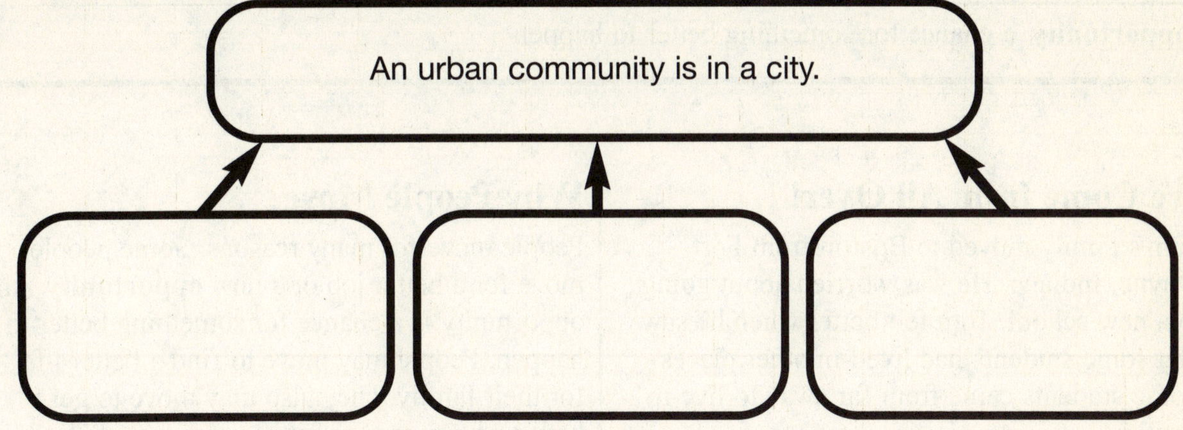

2. How is an urban community different from a rural community? How is it similar?

3. Name three fun things to do in Chicago.

4. Name one way that people in Chicago get around that is not found in rural communities.

5. **Critical Thinking: *Compare and Contrast*** How is a city similar to and different from its suburbs?

Name ____________________ Date __________ **Lesson 1 Summary**

Use with pages 74–77.

Lesson 1: Moving to a New Community

Vocabulary

opportunity a chance for something better to happen

We Come from All Over!

Tom's family moved to Boston from Fort Wayne, Indiana. He was worried about going to a new school. Tom felt better when he saw that some students had lived in other places. Some students came from far away to live in Boston.

Why People Move

People move for many reasons. Some people move for a better job or a new **opportunity.** An opportunity is a chance for something better to happen. People may move to find a better life for their family. They also may move to get a better education. For many years, people have moved to the United States to be free and safe. They want to be free to help choose the government. They want to be free to follow their religion. They also want to make their children's future better. People who came to the United States made new communities here. They formed new communities to feel safer. They also wanted a better life. They set up laws to keep everyone safe. When new people move to a community, they become part of it. They must obey the laws. They can get jobs. They also make friends and go to school like everyone else. When everyone follows the laws, the community is a safe place to live.

Name ______________________ Date ____________ **Lesson 1 Review**

Use with pages 74–77.

Lesson 1: Review

1. **Compare and Contrast** Fill in the diagram to compare and contrast reasons why people might move within the United States to reasons why people might move here from another country.

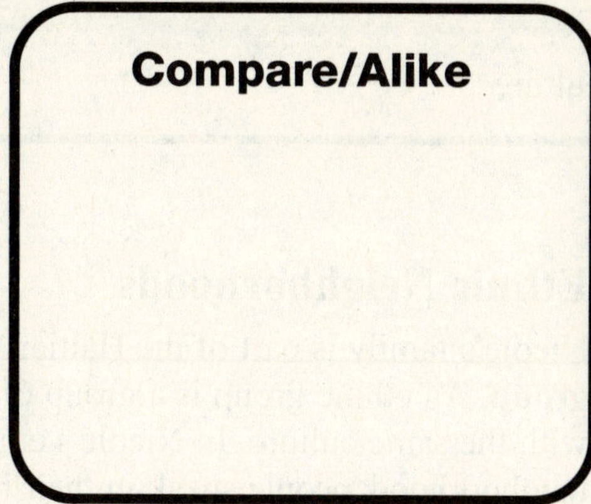

Contrast/Different

2. List reasons why people move to a new community.

____

____

____

3. Why have people formed new communities?

____

____

____

4. Why is it important for everyone to follow the laws of a community?

____

____

____

5. **Critical Thinking: *Draw Conclusions*** What are some of the things that you can do to keep your community a good place to live?

____

____

____

Name ______________________ Date ____________ **Lesson 2 Summary**

Use with pages 78–81.

Lesson 2: Learning New Customs

Vocabulary

immigrant a person who moves from one country to another to live

custom a way of doing things

ethnic group a group of people with the same culture

Moving to a New Country

Nicole's family moved to Boston, Massachusetts. They were from Haiti, a country in the Caribbean Sea. They moved to a community where other people from Haiti live. They are all **immigrants,** people who move to a new country to live. In Haiti Nicole's family spoke a language called Haitian Creole. Nicole's new friends helped her learn English. Her family still follows **customs,** or ways of doing things, from Haiti. Some things in Boston are the same as in Haiti. School is almost the same. Kids play soccer, ride buses, and also phone their friends. The neighborhood is different, though. Nicole lived in a rural community in Haiti. She lives in a city neighborhood in Boston.

Ethnic Neighborhoods

Nicole's family is part of the Haitian **ethnic group.** An ethnic group is a group of people with the same culture. In Nicole's ethnic neighborhood, people speak in their home language. They can eat the same kind of food they ate in Haiti. They can also follow the customs of Haiti. They can learn about a new culture while still doing things from their old culture.

Name ______________________ Date ____________ **Lesson 2 Review**

Use with pages 78–81.

Lesson 2: Review

1. **Compare and Contrast** Fill in the diagram comparing Nicole's old community to her new one.

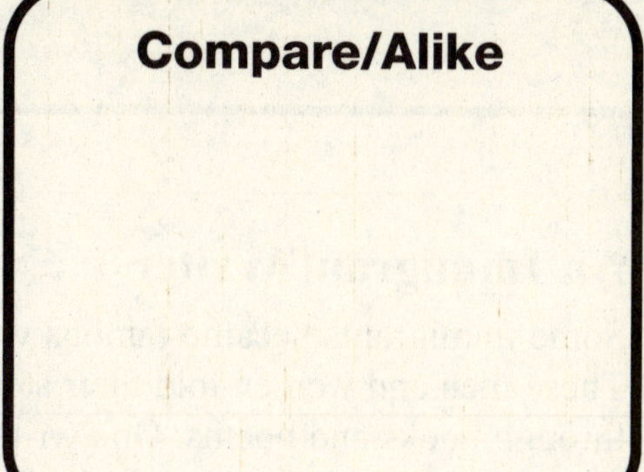

Contrast/Different

2. Why do you think Nicole's family moved to an ethnic neighborhood?

____

____

____

3. Give an example of how immigrants mix some of their old culture with their new culture.

____

____

____

4. What parts of their culture can immigrants find in an ethnic neighborhood?

____

____

____

5. **Critical Thinking: *Apply Information*** If you moved to a new country, what do you think would be the hardest thing to learn? What would be the easiest?

____

____

____

Name ________________ Date ________ **Lesson 3 Summary**

Use with pages 84–89.

Lesson 3: Where Did They Come From?

Vocabulary

ancestor a relative who lived long ago

symbol an object that stands for something else

They Came Long Ago

Nancy's **ancestors,** or relatives who lived long ago, were immigrants. They came to the United States from Europe in the early 1900s. Many other immigrants came around the same time. The first thing they saw was the Statue of Liberty in New York Bay. The statue was a **symbol** of freedom to the immigrants. A symbol is an object that stands for something else. The statue meant that their long trip was over. They could live in freedom in the United States.

A Nation of Immigrants

Immigrants have come to the United States from almost every other country in the world. They came for freedom or opportunities. Some came because there was little food in their home country. Some came to find jobs. Some immigrants were even forced to come. Many immigrants from Europe came into the United States through New York City. Many immigrants from Asia came through San Francisco, California.

An Immigrant Writer

Some immigrants became famous writers. These men and women told their stories through books and poems. One writer was Mary Antin. Mary came to the United States from Russia when she was twelve years old. Her family lived in Boston. She wrote a book, *The Promised Land,* about her life in Boston.

An Immigrant Artist

Some people who came to the United States became artists. These men and women made paintings and statues. They shared their artwork with other people. Emanuel Gottlieb Leutze was born in Germany. He came to the United States when he was nine years old. He lived in Philadelphia. His most famous painting is *Washington Crossing the Delaware.* It was painted in 1851. It shows George Washington during the Revolutionary War.

Name ______________________ Date __________ **Lesson 3 Review**

Use with pages 84–89.

Lesson 3: Review

1. **Main Idea and Details** Fill in the main idea.

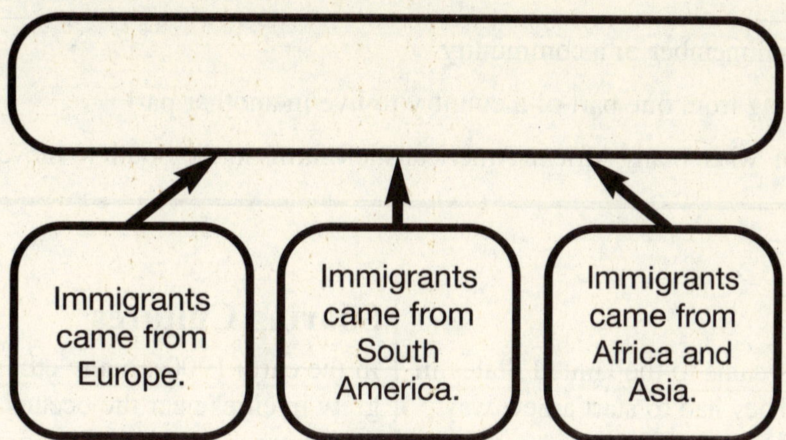

2. Why was the Statue of Liberty an important symbol to the immigrants?

____

____

____

3. Where have immigrants to the United States come from?

____

____

____

4. How have immigrant writers and artists shared their stories with the rest of the world?

____

____

____

5. **Critical Thinking: *Interpret Visuals*** Look at the painting on page 88 in your main book. Which man is George Washington? How can you tell that he is the leader?

____

____

____

Use with pages 90–95.

Lesson 4: A New Life in America

Vocabulary

citizen an official member of a community

migration moving from one part of a country to live in another part

Great Migration when many African Americans left farms in the South to move to the North

A New Life

Many immigrants came to the United States in the early 1900s. They had to start a new way of life. Many had to learn a new language. They also had to find homes and jobs. Some immigrants moved into ethnic neighborhoods in cities. Others worked on farms and lived in small towns. Most immigrants wanted to become citizens of the United States. A **citizen** is an official member of a country. Citizens can help make decisions for their community by voting.

Education Past and Present

Some immigrants came from places where schools were very different. In some countries, children started school at younger ages. They learned their country's language and history. In the United States, immigrant children were taught about the way of life and government of their new country. They learned math and science. Some even learned English for the first time. Even today, schools are different in different countries. Children who come to the United States today learn things that children of the past had to learn.

Sharing Cultures

In the early 1900s, many ethnic communities grew in cities near the oceans. As these neighborhoods grew, cities grew. Each group of immigrants brought their own customs. Later, the different customs started to mix together. The songs of one group were sung by others. People started to eat the foods of other ethnic groups. They played the games and sports of other groups.

Moving North

Many African Americans moved from the South to the North in the early 1900s. They wanted a better way of life. This was called the **Great Migration. Migration** means moving from one part of a country to live in another part. Many African Americans left farms in the South. They moved to northern cities, such as New York City, New York; Chicago, Illinois; and Pittsburgh, Pennsylvania. They hoped to get good jobs in the factories there. When they moved, African Americans brought their culture with them. Many were musicians, writers, and artists. Some of their work became famous.

Name ______________________ Date ____________ **Lesson 4 Review**

Use with pages 90–95.

Lesson 4: Review

1. **Main Idea and Details** Fill in the main idea.

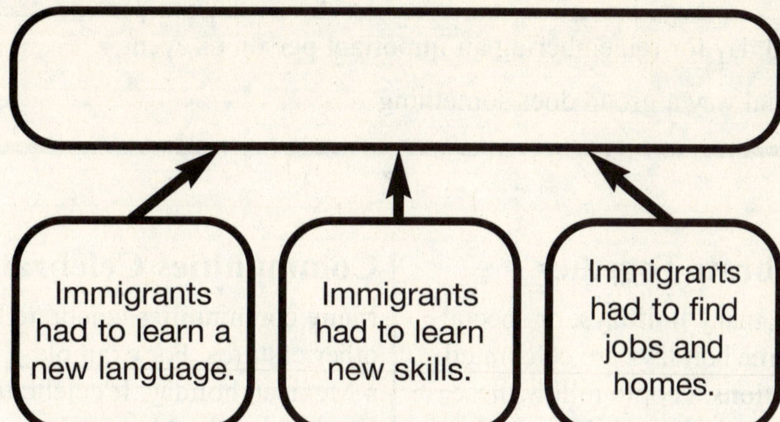

2. How can a citizen in the United States help make decisions for the community?

____

____

____

3. How were schools in other countries different from those in the United States?

____

____

____

4. Why did many African Americans move from the South to the North during the Great Migration?

____

____

____

5. **Critical Thinking: *Draw Conclusions*** Explain how people from different cultures can help make a community special.

____

____

____

Name ______________________ Date ____________ **Lesson 1 Summary**

Use with pages 104–109.

Lesson 1: Celebrating Cultures

Vocabulary

holiday a special day for remembering an important person or event

tradition a special way a group does something

Families Celebrate Together

Families celebrate many **holidays,** or special days, together. Some holidays are celebrated with certain **traditions.** People follow these traditions every year during a celebration. Traditions help people feel that they are part of a community. One tradition for many Asian families is to have a certain meal for Asian New Year. Some Asian communities also celebrate fall moon festivals.

Family Celebrations

Some holidays, such as Christmas and Hanukkah, are religious. Others are not. On many holidays, families eat a meal together. Many holidays have traditions, symbols, and music. Cakes with candles are symbols that are often used to celebrate birthdays. Some families celebrate Christmas. They light candles and go to church. Many give gifts to family members. Muslim families celebrate Eid-al-Fitr. They eat a meal and special sweets. Many children get gifts. Many Jewish families celebrate Hanukkah. They light candles for eight nights. Families eat special foods. Some African American families celebrate Kwanzaa. They light seven candles. Each candle stands for something special.

Communities Celebrate Cultures

Many communities celebrate holidays from other cultures. For example, Cinco de Mayo is a Mexican holiday. It celebrates a special day. On this day the Mexicans won a battle against the French. Many people around the world celebrate Cinco de Mayo. They wear colorful clothes. They play music and eat Mexican food. St. Patrick's Day is another holiday. It is celebrated in many places. It began as a religious holiday in Ireland. This is a day to celebrate Irish culture. Some people wear green clothes. They may go to a parade or eat green food.

Use with pages 104–109.

Lesson 1: Review

1. **Compare and Contrast** Fill in the diagram with more facts to compare and contrast family celebrations and community celebrations.

Compare/Alike	Contrast/Different

2. Why do people celebrate holidays?

3. Why do groups of people follow traditions?

4. Tell how people in other countries and in the United States celebrate ethnic holidays such as Cinco de Mayo and St. Patrick's Day.

5. **Critical Thinking: *Apply Information*** Tell how you celebrate events that are important to you.

Use with pages 114–117.

Lesson 2: Celebrating a Community's Past

Vocabulary

livestock farm animals raised on local farms

Community Celebrations

Many communities have celebrations for important people or events. These celebrations help bring the community together. One example of a community celebration is a fair. Communities hold community fairs or state fairs. These fairs bring community members together. Some communities hold heritage festivals. These festivals honor the history and culture of the people who live there. New Orleans, Louisiana, has a famous heritage festival. Some communities celebrate Founder's Day. This day honors the people who started the community.

Kansas State Fair

State fairs celebrate the work people have done all year. People from all over Kansas show their best work at the state fair. The state fair is held in September. That is when the crops are ready to eat. Farmers bring **livestock,** or farm animals, to show. Other people show homemade arts and crafts. Some show plants, vegetables, and baked goods. People judge many of these things. The winners get ribbons.

Remembering Their Past

Some communities celebrate events from long ago. Many Native American groups celebrate the Green Corn Festival. Groups such as the Cherokee, Creek, and Seminole gather to dance, play games, and continue a tradition started long ago.

Name ______________________ Date ____________ **Lesson 2 Review**

Use with pages 114–117.

Lesson 2: Review

1. **Compare and Contrast** Fill in the diagram with facts to compare and contrast kinds of community celebrations.

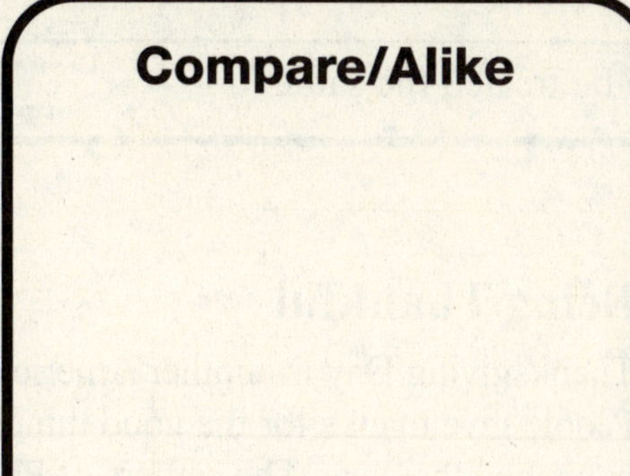

Contrast/Different

2. Why do some communities have a heritage festival?

____

____

____

3. When do state fairs usually take place?

____

____

____

4. What is one reason why state fairs take place?

____

____

____

5. **Critical Thinking: *Apply Information*** Why do communities celebrate their history?

____

____

____

Name ______________________ Date __________ **Lesson 3 Summary**

Use with pages 120–123.

Lesson 3: Celebrations Across Our Nation

Vocabulary

Civil Rights Movement a drive for all people to be treated the same

Holidays for Freedom

Many holidays honor freedom in the United States. Independence Day celebrates the founding of our country. Memorial Day honors people who fought and died in wars for freedom. Veterans Day honors people who fought for freedom. Martin Luther King Day also celebrates a fight for freedom. Dr. King led the **Civil Rights Movement.** This was a drive for all people to be treated the same. Dr. King used words to fight. He did not believe in violence. He wanted fair treatment of African Americans.

Being Thankful

Thanksgiving Day is another American holiday. People give thanks for the good things that happened that year. The settlers of Plymouth, Massachusetts, celebrated one of the first Thanksgivings in 1621. These settlers were called Pilgrims. Pilgrims had come from England to be free to practice their own religion. Their first winter had been very hard. The next fall, the Pilgrims wanted to give thanks to God. They were thankful for their good crops and for living through the winter. They also wanted to thank a group of Wampanoag Indians who had helped them. Today, we give thanks for what we have. Families celebrate by having a special meal together.

Name ________________ Date ________ **Lesson 3 Review**

Use with pages 120–123.

Lesson 3: Review

1. **Main Idea and Details** Fill in the diagram to show more details about the main idea.

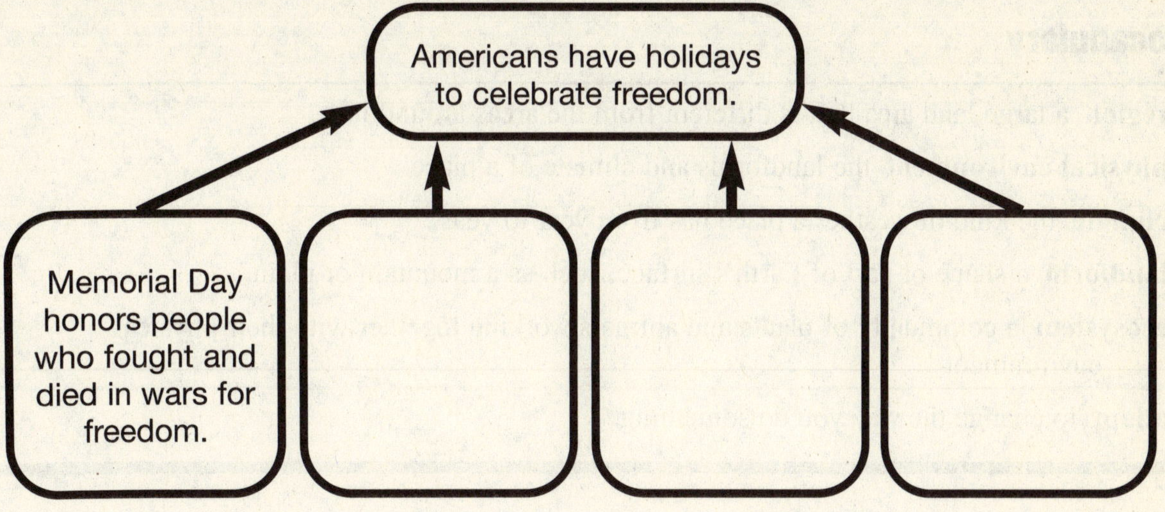

2. What was the Civil Rights Movement?

____

____

____

3. How did Dr. Martin Luther King, Jr., try to make changes in the United States?

____

____

____

4. Why did the Pilgrims come to America?

____

____

____

5. **Critical Thinking: *Make Inferences*** Why did the Pilgrims need help from the Wampanoag?

____

____

____

Name ______________________ Date __________ **Lesson 1 Summary**

Use with pages 142–147.

Lesson 1: What Is Your Community's Environment?

Vocabulary

region a large land area that is different from the areas around it

physical environment the landforms and climate of a place

climate the kind of weather a place has from year to year

landform a shape or part of Earth's surface, such as a mountain or plain

ecosystem a community of plants and animals working together with their physical environment

adapt to change the way you do something

Katrinka's Western Community

Katrinka lives in Bozeman, Montana. Katrinka walks in the nearby mountains. She likes to fish in the nearby rivers. Montana is in the Western **region** of the United States. A region is a large land area. Each region is special. Regions have different **landforms.** Landforms are parts of Earth's surface. Mountains and plains are landforms. Regions also have different **climates.** Climate is the kind of weather a place has from year to year. A region's landforms and climate are part of its **physical environment.**

Communities in the Regions

People live in communities in all regions of the United States. The land around each community looks different. Different plants and animals live in each region. The land, plants, and animals form an **ecosystem.** In an ecosystem, plants and animals work together with their physical environment. A river is a kind of ecosystem. So are a forest and a desert. People use the physical environments of their communities. Stamford, Connecticut, is in the Northeast region. People walk in the nearby hills and forests. They may see deer and snakes. Charleston, South Carolina, is in the Southeast region. People there ride boats on rivers. They may see rice fields and birds. There also are many trees. Omaha, Nebraska, is in the Midwest region. There also are rivers in this area. People ride bikes on the flat land. They sometimes hear coyotes. Tucson, Arizona, is in the Southwest region. People there see canyons, deserts, rivers, and mountains. They can walk in parks. They may see cactuses, snakes, and desert toads.

Changes in People and Places

People **adapt** to their physical environment. Adapt means to change the way you do something. Adapting helps people live in certain places. In cold places, people heat buildings and wear warm clothes. People also change the environment to meet their needs. They cut down trees and forests to build houses. They build roads to move people and goods. People build cities and railroads. They bring water to very dry places to grow crops.

Name ______________________ Date ____________ **Lesson 1 Review**

Use with pages 142–147.

Lesson 1: Review

1. **Draw Conclusions** Choose a community from this lesson. Use the details you read about to draw a conclusion about how the physical environment affects life in the community.

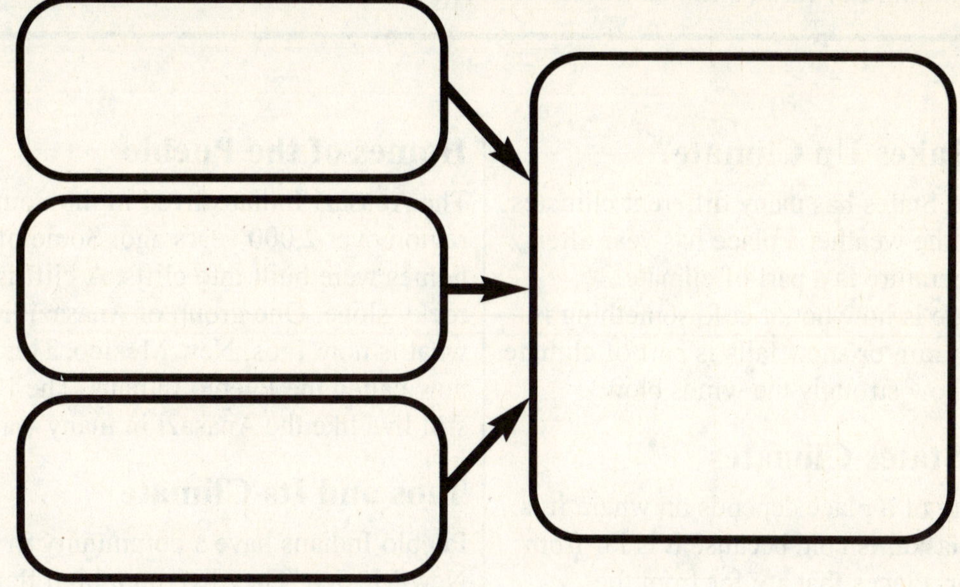

2. What makes up the physical environment of a region?

____

____

3. List five regions of the United States and tell about their physical environments.

____

____

4. How do people adapt to and change their environment?

____

____

5. **Critical Thinking:** ***Predict*** How might building a large new highway affect a rural community?

____

____

Name ______________________ Date ____________ **Lesson 2 Summary**

Use with pages 150–155.

Lesson 2: Living in Different Climates

Vocabulary

adobe a mixture of earth, straw, and water that is made into bricks and dried

What Makes Up Climate?

The United States has many different climates. Climate is the weather a place has year after year. Temperature is a part of climate. Temperature is how hot or cold something is. How much rain or snow falls is part of climate too. So is how strongly the winds blow.

United States Climates

The climate of a place depends on where it is. Barrow, Alaska, is cold because it is far from the equator. Places that are far from the equator are cold. Places that are near the equator are warm. Kauai, Hawaii, is near the equator. It is warm all year. The climate of a place also depends on how high it is. Very high places can be cold. Mountains can have snow all year. Being near very large lakes or oceans may also affect climates. People adapt to their climate. They wear clothes to keep them cool or warm. They build homes that keep them safe.

Homes of the Pueblo

The Anasazi Indians lived in the Southwest region over 2,000 years ago. Some of their homes were built into cliffs. A cliff is a steep, rocky slope. One group of Anasazi lived in what is now Taos, New Mexico. This group is now called the Pueblo Indians. The Pueblo still live like the Anasazi in many ways.

Taos and Its Climate

Pueblo Indians have a community in Taos, New Mexico. They live on a high flat area with mountains around it. The climate is dry. In summer, Taos has warm days and cool nights. In winter, the weather can be cold. Snow falls often. The Pueblo adapted to this climate. They built houses from **adobe.** Adobe is a mixture of earth, straw, and water. It is made into bricks and dried. Adobe houses keep people warm in winter and cool in summer.

Name ______________________ Date ____________ **Lesson 2 Review**

Use with pages 150–155.

Lesson 2: Review

1. **Draw Conclusions** Use details to draw a conclusion about how you adapt to the climate where you live.

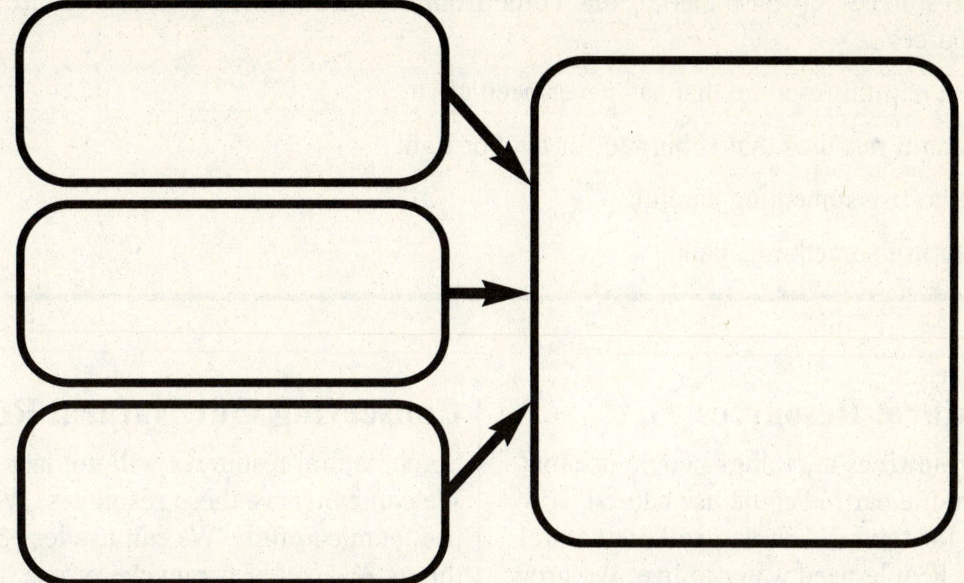

2. What are the different parts of the climate of a place?

____

____

3. What causes the climate of some places to be warm and other places to be cold?

____

____

4. How have people in the Pueblo Indian community in Taos, New Mexico, adapted to the climate?

____

____

5. **Critical Thinking: *Evaluate*** In which type of climate would you rather live? Why?

____

____

Name ______________________ Date ______________ **Lesson 3 Summary**

Use with pages 160–165.

Lesson 3: Communities and Resources

Vocabulary

natural resources useful materials that come from the earth; water, soil, and oil are natural resources

mineral a natural resource that has never been alive

fuel a natural resource that is burned for heat or light

conserve to use something carefully

recycle to use something again

Our Natural Resources

Natural resources are things people use that come from the earth. People use natural resources for food. Water and soil are natural resources. People need water to live. We grow food in soil. Natural resources such as trees are used to build homes. **Minerals** are natural resources that were never alive. Gold and salt are minerals. **Fuels** are natural resources too. A fuel is something that is burned for heat or light. Oil and gas are fuels.

Mineral Resources

In 1848 gold was found in California. Thousands of people rushed there. They wanted to find gold. This movement was called the Gold Rush. People looked for gold in muddy streams. They dug deep into the earth. Many people stayed in communities in California after the Gold Rush ended. Oil is another important natural resource. In 1901 oil was found in Beaumont, Texas. Many people moved to this Texas community. They wanted to work in the oil fields. Oil is still important in Texas today. Alaska is another state where oil is important. People use oil to make motor oil and gasoline for cars. People also use oil to make plastics.

Conserving Our Natural Resources

Some natural resources will not last forever. We can **conserve** these resources. We should use them carefully. We can use less of some things. We can also **recycle,** or use things again. Some things can be recycled and made into new products. Paper is one of these things. We can take better care of some resources, such as soil. Fuels are natural resources that can be used up. We can conserve fuels by using them carefully.

Use with pages 160–165.

Lesson 3: Review

1. **Draw Conclusions** Use the details you read about to draw a conclusion about the importance of conserving natural resources.

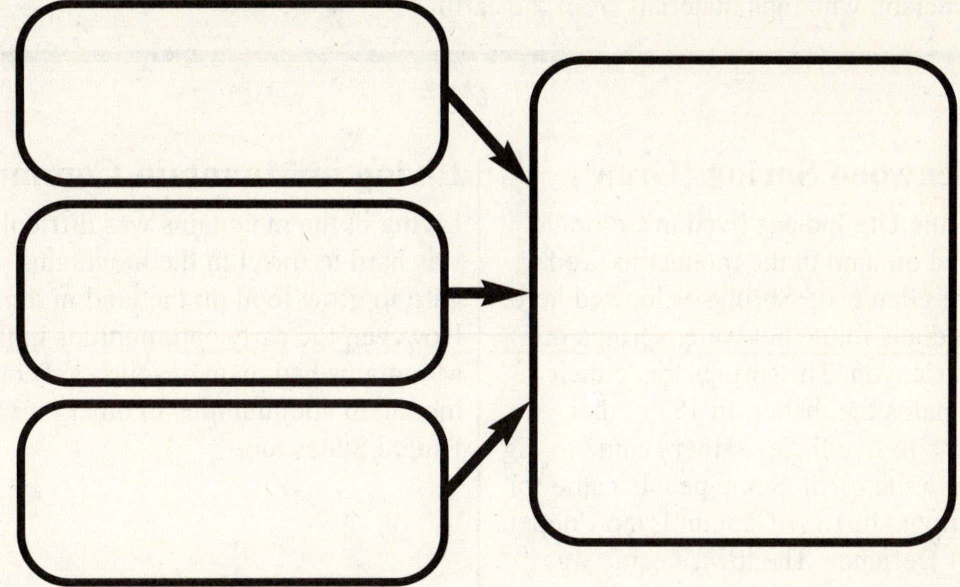

2. Describe some important natural resources.

____

____

3. How has the discovery of natural resources changed communities?

____

____

4. What are some ways that people can conserve resources?

____

____

5. **Critical Thinking:** ***Observe*** Why do you think the use of oil has increased since 1901?

____

____

Name ______________________ Date ____________ **Lesson 1 Summary**

Use with pages 172–175.

Lesson 1: A Mountain Community

Vocabulary

miner a person who digs materials from the earth

How Glenwood Springs Grew

Long ago, the Ute Indians lived in Colorado. They settled on land in the mountains. Today, the town of Glenwood Springs is located here. The Ute Indians found hot water springs in Glenwood Canyon. The springs made their aches and pains feel better. In 1879 other people came to live there. **Miners** came to dig up coal from the earth. Some people came for the hot springs. In 1881 Captain Isaac Cooper set up Fort Defiance. The town's name was changed to Glenwood Springs. In 1887 the railroad came through the Rocky Mountains to Glenwood Springs. This gave miners a way to send out coal. People also rode the train to visit the hot springs.

Living in Mountain Communities

Living in the mountains was difficult. It was hard to travel in the mountains. It was hard to grow food on the land in mountains. However, the early communities in the Rocky Mountains had many resources. People started mountain communities in other parts of the United States too.

Name ______________________ Date ____________ **Lesson 1 Review**

Use with pages 172–175.

Lesson 1: Review

1. **Draw Conclusions** Use the details you read about Glenwood Springs. Draw a conclusion about why people settled there.

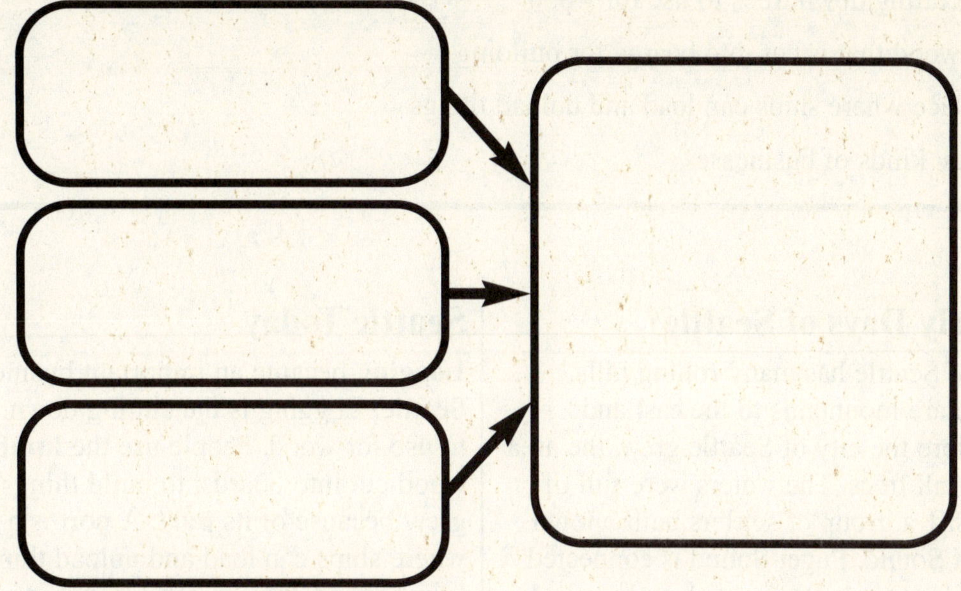

2. What events changed Glenwood Springs over time?

____

____

3. What natural resource brings visitors to Glenwood Springs?

____

____

4. What made it difficult to live in mountain communities?

____

____

5. **Critical Thinking: *Compare and Contrast*** Why did the Utes and the settlers come to the Glenwood Springs area? How were their reasons similar and different?

____

____

Name ______________________ Date __________

Lesson 2 Summary

Use with pages 178–181.

Lesson 2: A Water Community

Vocabulary

logging cutting down trees to use for wood

lumber wood that is cut into boards for building

port a place where ships can load and unload things

industries kinds of businesses

The Early Days of Seattle

The city of Seattle has many rolling hills. There also are mountains to the east and south. Before the city of Seattle grew, the area had many tall trees. The waters were full of fish. In 1851 a group of settlers built a town near Puget Sound. Puget Sound is connected to the Pacific Ocean. Duwamish and Suquamish Indians lived in the area. One of the Native American leaders was Chief Sealth. He was friendly to settlers and helped them. The settlers named their town Seattle after Chief Sealth. People told tall tales about how Puget Sound was formed. One of these stories is about a giant man named Paul Bunyan. The story says that Bunyan dug out land to make Puget Sound.

Seattle Today

Logging became an important business in Seattle. Logging is the cutting down of trees to use for wood. People use the **lumber,** or wood cut into boards, to build things. Seattle grew because of its **port.** A port is a place where ships can load and unload things. Lumber and other goods were shipped to and from Seattle. New **industries** have come to Seattle. Industries are kinds of businesses. Today, Seattle is known for airplane making and computer companies. Some people now worry about what will happen to Seattle's natural resources.

Name ______________________ Date ______________ **Lesson 2 Review**

Use with pages 178–181.

Lesson 2: Review

1. **Draw Conclusions** Use the details you read about Seattle. Draw a conclusion about the good and bad effects of Seattle's growth.

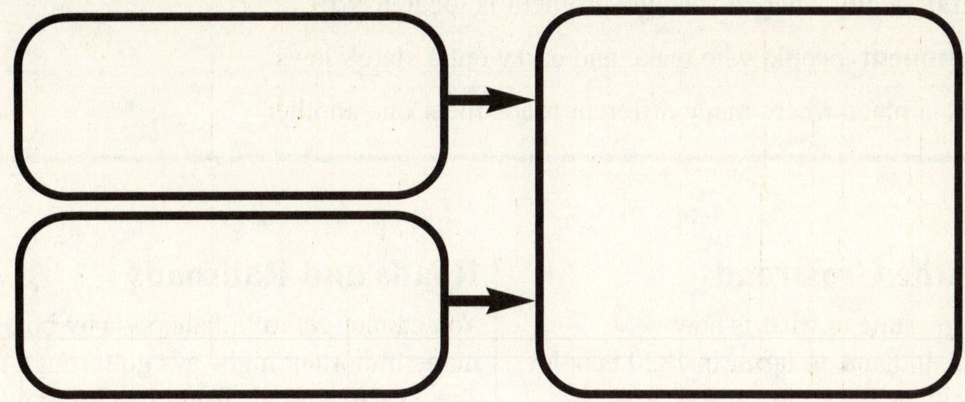

2. Describe a person and an event that changed Seattle.

____

____

____

3. Describe the physical environment and the natural resources around Seattle.

____

____

____

4. In what way were wood and water important natural resources in the growth of Seattle?

____

____

____

5. **Critical Thinking: *Predict*** How do you think Seattle will change if its population continues to grow quickly?

____

____

____

Name ______________________ Date ____________ **Lesson 3 Summary**

Use with pages 186–189.

Lesson 3: A Crossroads Community

Vocabulary

state capital a city where a state government is located

state government people who make and carry out a state's laws

crossroads a place where many different roads meet one another

Forming the Crossroads

White settlers came to what is now Indianapolis, Indiana, to farm. In 1820 people picked the city as the **state capital.** A state capital is a city where the **state government** is located. People in state government make and carry out a state's laws. In the 1830s the first highway in the United States came through Indianapolis. The highway was called the National Road. It helped people move from east to west. More roads were built. Indianapolis became known as the "Crossroads of America." A **crossroads** is a place where many different roads meet.

Roads and Railroads

You cannot get to Indianapolis by boat. But many important highways go through the city. Trucks carry goods from the city to other parts of the country. The railroad came to Indianapolis in 1847. It brought many people to Indianapolis. The Union Rail Station was built in 1852. Indianapolis became an important stop for many railroad lines. The **Underground Railroad** also stopped in Indianapolis. It was not a real railroad. It was a way for African American slaves to get to freedom in the North. The Underground Railroad was made up of a group of places for people to stop. One stop was Bethel AME Church in Indianapolis. Some people in the church helped the slaves escape.

Name ______________________ Date ____________ **Lesson 3 Review**

Use with pages 186–189.

Lesson 3: Review

1. **Draw Conclusions** Use details from the lesson. Draw a conclusion about the importance of Indianapolis in the past and present.

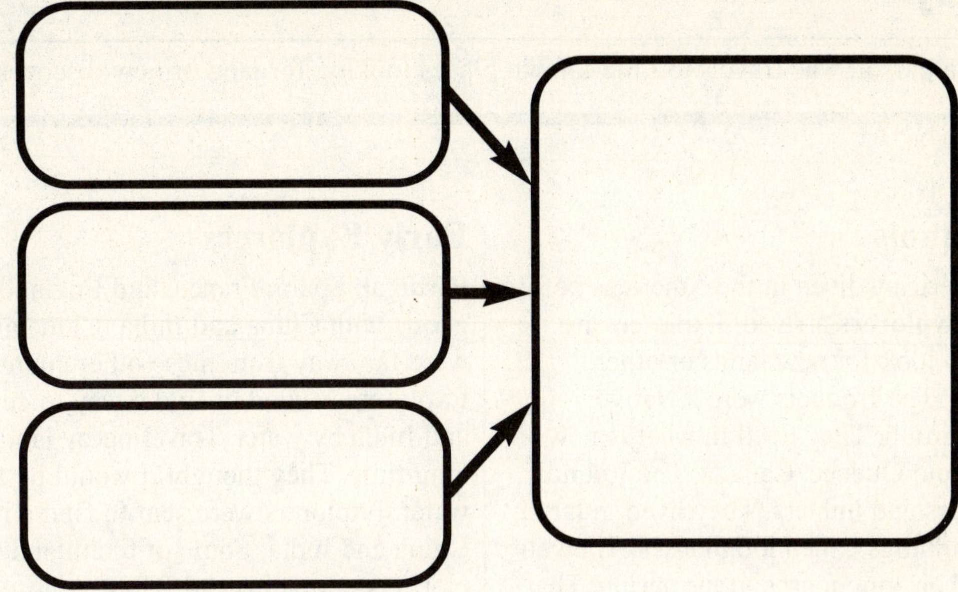

2. Why is Indianapolis known as the "Crossroads of America"?

____

____

3. What events were important to Indianapolis's early growth?

____

____

4. What made Indianapolis an important stop on the Underground Railroad?

____

____

5. **Critical Thinking: *Evaluate*** Why do you think so many roads were built through Indianapolis?

____

____

Name ______________________ Date ______________ **Lesson 1 Summary**

Use with pages 208–211.

Lesson 1: Explorers Come to North America

Vocabulary

explorer a person who travels to little-known places looking for land or new discoveries

The Iroquois

Native Americans lived in the Americas before European **explorers** arrived. Explorers are people who look for new lands or other discoveries. The Iroquois were a Native American group. They lived in what is now New York and Quebec, Canada. The Iroquois were farmers and hunters. They lived in large, wooden buildings called longhouses. They cut wood for their longhouses in the spring. That was when the wood was green and easy to bend. The Iroquois had a government. They had rules that protected the rights of their people. The rules also protected their ways of worship. In time, explorers from Spain, England, and France came to the Americas. The Europeans had different beliefs and ideas from the Native Americans. The differences sometimes led to problems.

Early Explorers

Portugal, Spain, France, and England traded goods with China and India. China and India were far away from these other countries. Explorers wanted to find a way to get to China and India by water. Traveling by land took a long time. They thought it would be faster by water. Explorers were sent to find a route to China and India. Some of them landed in North America instead. They explored North America. Some built settlements. Some people who explored North America for Spain were Christopher Columbus, Hernando de Soto, and Juan Ponce de León. French explorers were Jacques Cartier and Samuel de Champlain. England sent John Cabot and Henry Hudson.

Name ______________________ Date ______________ **Lesson 1 Review**

Use with pages 208–211.

Lesson 1: Review

1. **Cause and Effect** Fill in the effects for each of the causes.

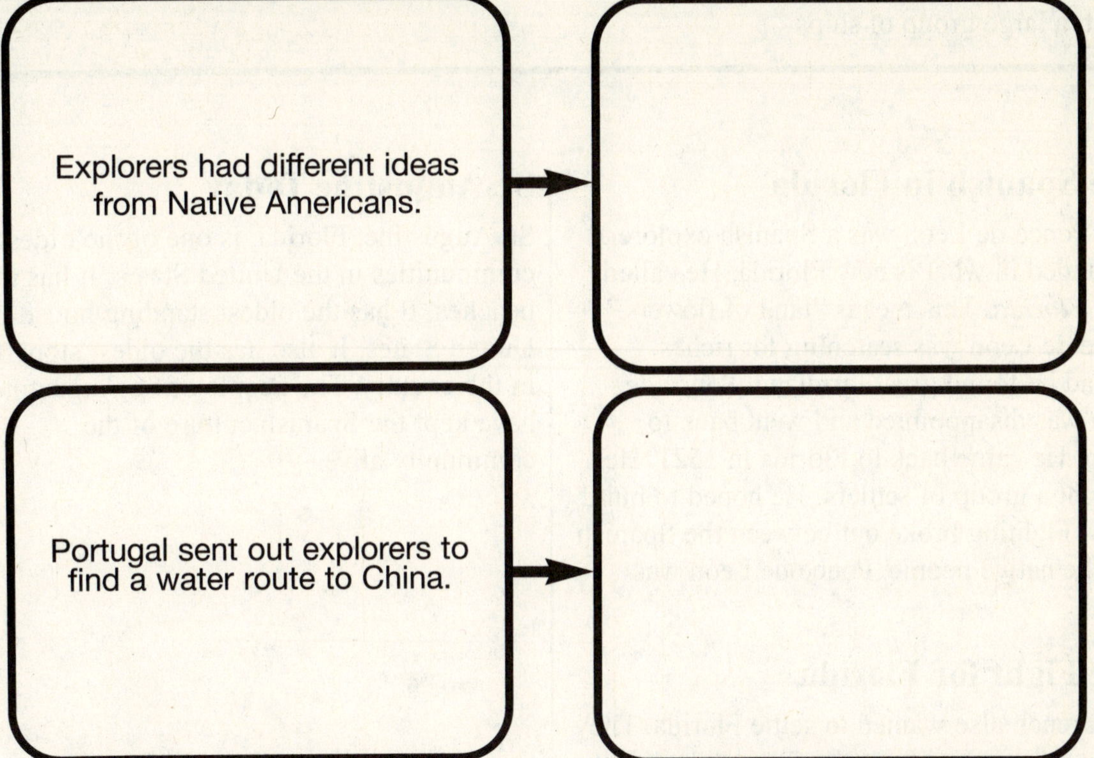

2. Why did the Iroquois cut wood for their houses in the spring?

____

____

3. What rights did the Iroquois form of government protect?

____

____

4. Name four countries that sent explorers to the Americas.

____

____

5. **Critical Thinking: *Draw Conclusions*** Why do you think that the countries that traded with China and India wanted a water route to those countries?

____

____

Use with pages 214–219.

Lesson 2: A Spanish Community

Vocabulary

fleet a large group of ships

The Spanish in Florida

Juan Ponce de León was a Spanish explorer. He landed in what is now Florida. He called it *La Florida.* This means "land of flowers." Ponce de León was searching for riches. Instead he found great farmland. Ponce de León was disappointed and went back to Spain. He came back to Florida in 1521. He brought a group of settlers. He hoped to build a city. Fighting broke out between the Spanish and the native people. Ponce de León was killed.

The Fight for Florida

The French also wanted to settle Florida. They set up a fort near where the Spanish had first landed. The king of Spain sent Don Pedro Menéndez de Avilés to explore and settle Florida. Menéndez and his settlers built a fort and settlement. They named it St. Augustine. The French and Spanish fought to control the coast of Florida. The Spanish took the French fort. They also defeated the French **fleet,** or group of ships. St. Augustine became the first permanent European settlement in North America.

St. Augustine Today

St. Augustine, Florida, is one of the oldest communities in the United States. It has many beaches. It has the oldest standing house in the United States. It also has the oldest stone fort in the country. The people of St. Augustine have kept the Spanish culture of the community alive.

Name ______________________ Date ____________ **Lesson 2 Review**

Use with pages 214–219.

Lesson 2: Review

1. **Cause and Effect** For each cause, fill in the effect in the correct box.

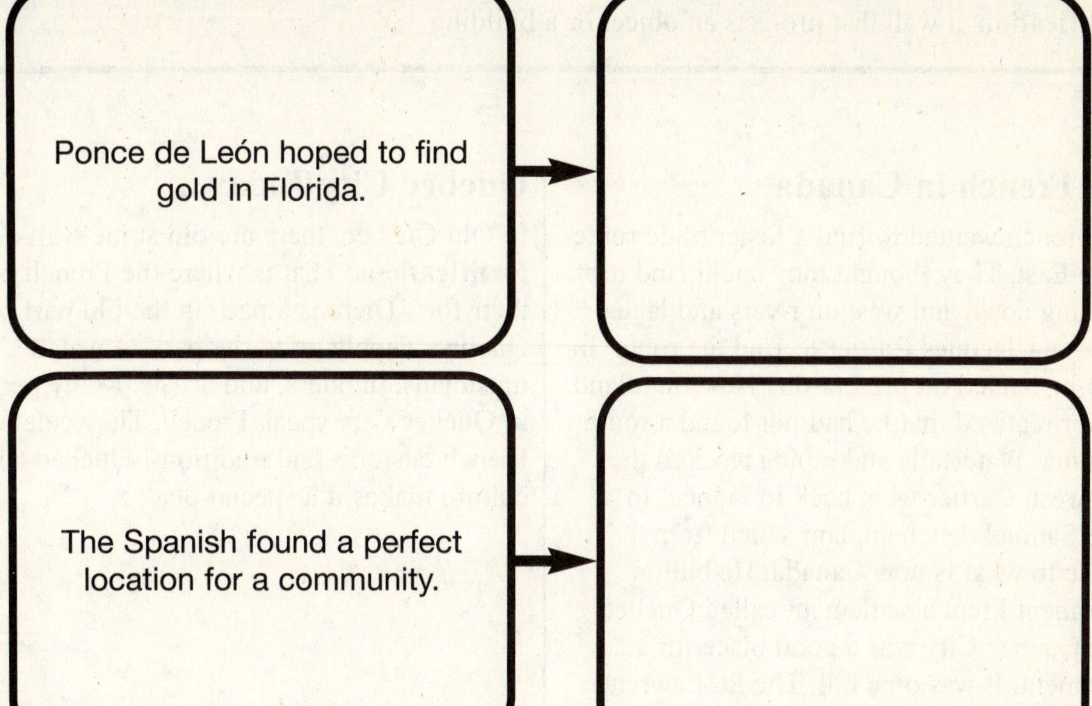

2. What does *La Florida* mean in English?

____

____

3. Why did Ponce de León come back to Florida in 1521?

____

____

4. What two countries fought over Florida in the 1500s?

____

____

5. **Critical Thinking: *Draw Conclusions*** How can you tell that people who live in St. Augustine today are proud of their history?

____

____

Use with pages 224–227.

Lesson 3: A French Community

Vocabulary

fortification a wall that protects an object or a building

The French in Canada

The French wanted to find a faster trade route to the East. They thought they could find it by traveling north and west on rivers and lakes. They sent Jacques Cartier to find the route. In 1534 he landed on present-day Newfoundland. Cartier realized that he had not found a route to China. Waterfalls and rapids blocked the path west. Cartier went back to France. In 1608 Samuel de Champlain sailed from France to what is now Canada. He built a permanent French settlement called Quebec City. Quebec City was a good place for a settlement. It was on a hill. The St. Lawrence River was good for travel and trade. During the next 150 years, many battles were fought for Quebec City. In 1759 the English took over. French rule in Canada ended.

Quebec City Today

In Old Quebec, there are old stone walls, or **fortifications.** That is where the French built their fort. There is a park in the old part of Quebec. People go to the park to watch musicians, jugglers, and artists. Many people in Quebec City speak French. They celebrate French customs and traditions. Quebec City's culture makes it a special place.

Name ______________________ Date ____________

Use with pages 224–227.

Lesson 3: Review

1. **Cause and Effect** Look at the cause. Fill in the effect in the box.

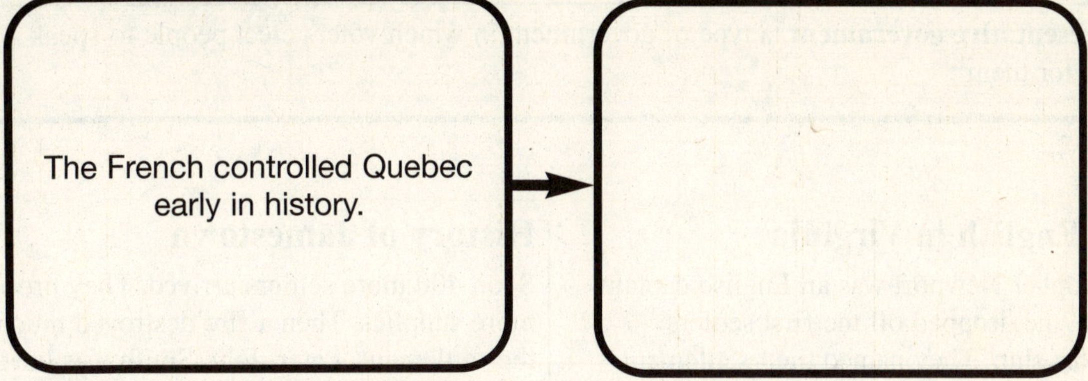

2. Why did Champlain build a permanent settlement at Quebec City?

____

____

3. Where did Cartier first land when he arrived in the Americas?

____

____

4. What culture makes Quebec City special?

____

____

5. **Critical Thinking: *Make Inferences*** Why would rapids and waterfalls cause Cartier to turn back from his search for a route to China and India?

____

____

Name ______________________ Date ____________ **Lesson 4 Summary**

Use with pages 230–235.

Lesson 4: An English Community

Vocabulary

representative government a type of government in which voters elect people to speak for them

The English in Virginia

Christopher Newport was an English captain. In 1607 he dropped off the first settlers from his ship. They named their settlement Jamestown. The settlers came to find riches. But they faced problems. They quickly ran out of food. John Smith was a leader in the settlement. He went to look for food. Native Americans had lived in this place for a long time. The Native American chief, Powhatan, agreed to help the settlers. Smith went back to the settlement. But only about 38 people out of 105 were still alive. The others had died of hunger or disease.

History of Jamestown

Soon 400 more settlers arrived. They brought more supplies. Then a fire destroyed much of the settlement. Later, John Smith was hurt. He went back to England. From September 1609 to May 1610, the settlement faced "the starving time." Many people died because they had no food. But then another ship landed and saved the town. The men in Jamestown had the same rights they had in England. One of these rights let them have a say in how they were governed. In 1619 settlers held the first representative assembly, a type of meeting. They met to form a **representative government.** In a representative government, voters elect leaders. The leaders speak for the people. The Jamestown government worked for all the people of Virginia.

Jamestown Today

Jamestown is a national historic site. People from all over the world come to visit. They want to learn the history of this important settlement.

Lesson 4: Review

1. **Cause and Effect** For each cause, fill in the effect in the correct box.

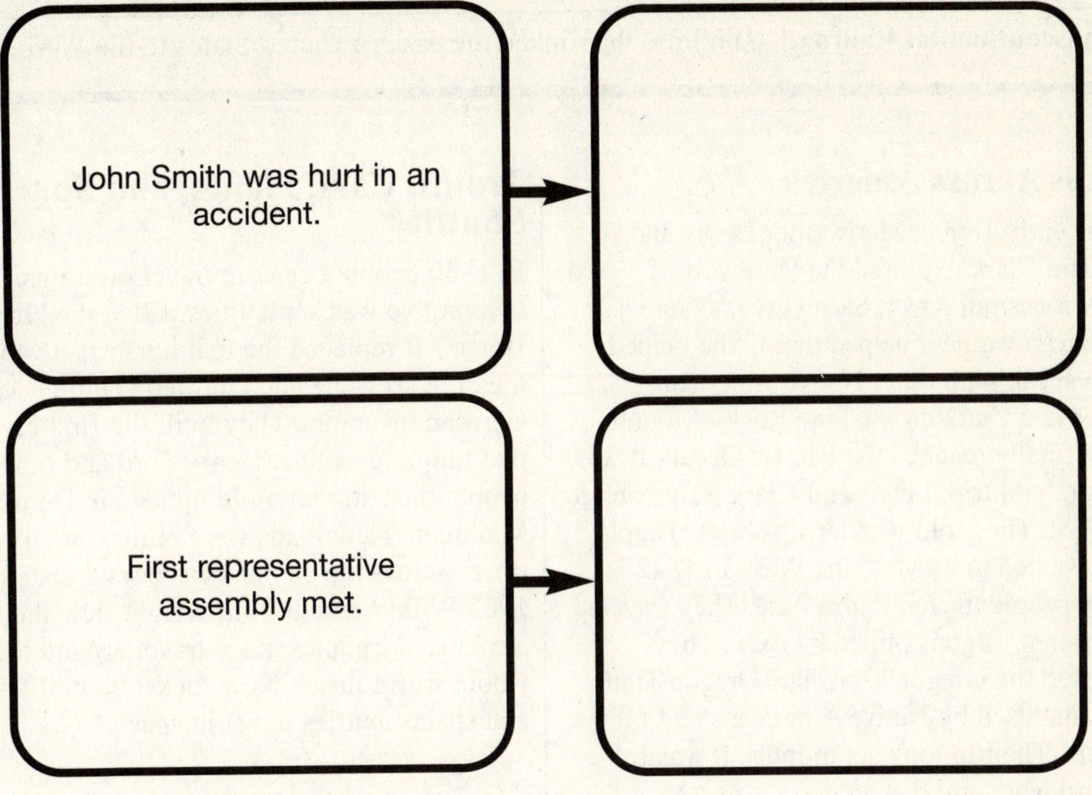

2. How did Christopher Newport help found Jamestown?

____

____

3. What was "the starving time"?

____

____

4. What was one right that some of the men brought with them to Jamestown?

____

____

5. **Critical Thinking: *Make Inferences*** Do you think that the settlers who came to Jamestown were prepared? Why or why not?

____

____

Name _______________ Date _______________ **Lesson 1 Summary**

Use with pages 242–247.

Lesson 1: Transportation Over Time

Vocabulary

Transcontinental Railroad train lines that linked the eastern United States to the West

Trails Across America

In the early 1800s, Meriwether Lewis and William Clark explored the land west of the Mississippi River. Sacagawea, a Native American woman, helped them. She helped them speak with other Native Americans. Lewis and Clark crossed the Rocky Mountains. They finally reached the Pacific Ocean. It was a long, hard trip. Lewis and Clark went back to the East. They told wonderful stories. People then wanted to move to the West. In 1842 many people moved to the West. They traveled in covered wagons pulled by oxen. They followed the Oregon Trail. The Oregon Trail was first used by Native Americans and fur traders. The trip took six months. It was full of hard work and danger.

Westward Expansion

More people headed west. They wanted to find riches. Families joined together in wagon trains. But people needed a better, safer way to travel. The steam locomotive changed the way people traveled. Soon railroad companies began to lay tracks across the country. In 1869 the **Transcontinental Railroad** was finished. This railway linked the eastern United States to the West.

Trains, Cars, Planes, and Space Shuttles

In 1830 people began to travel on trains. The locomotive was sometimes called the "Iron Horse." It replaced the real horse as a way to travel. Karl Benz and Gottlieb Daimler were German inventors. They built the first cars that ran on gasoline. Henry Ford and other people then started building cars in Detroit, Michigan. New roads were built. Cars made travel across the country easier and faster. In 1903 Wilbur and Orville Wright flew the first airplane. Airplanes made travel around the whole world faster. Now rockets, satellites, and space shuttles travel in space.

Lesson 1: Review

1. **Cause and Effect** For each cause, fill in the effect in the correct box.

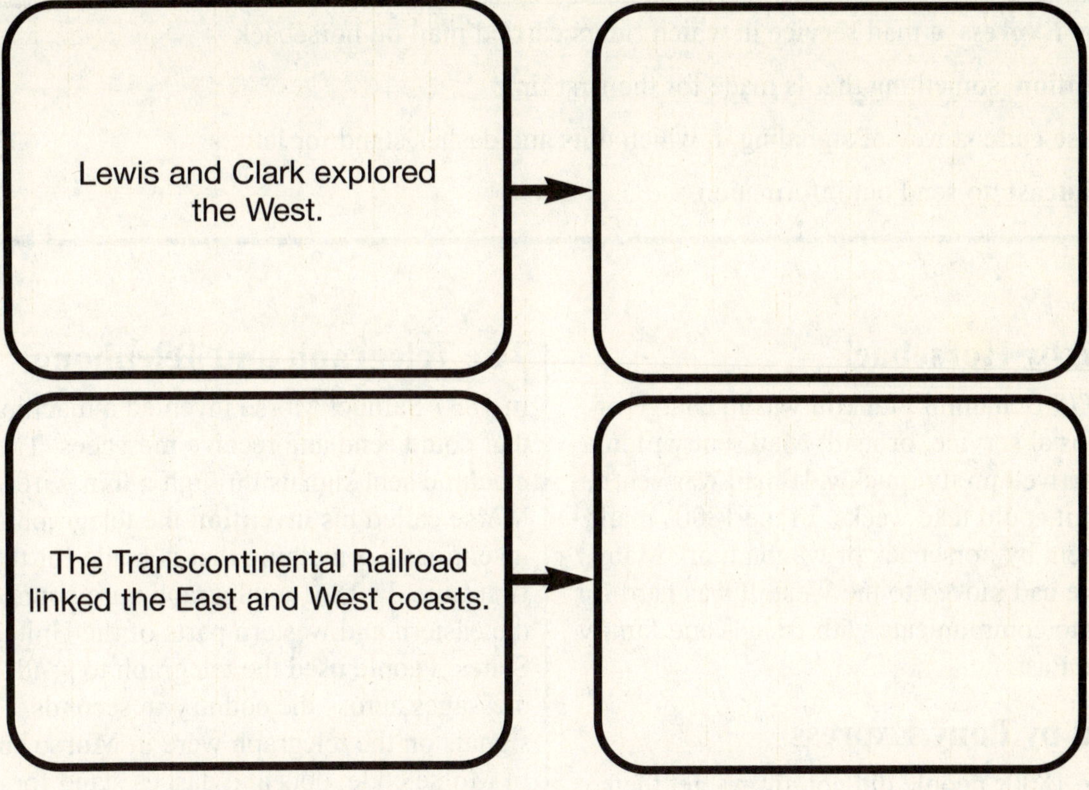

2. Which group of people first traveled along the Oregon Trail?

____

____

3. How did families traveling to the West on the Oregon Trail move their belongings?

____

____

4. What new form of transportation was the result of an invention by Orville and Wilbur Wright?

____

____

5. **Critical Thinking: *Make Inferences*** Why do you think the Iron Horse replaced the real horse as a way to travel to the West?

____

____

Name ______________________ Date ____________ **Lesson 2 Summary**

Use with pages 250–255.

Lesson 2: Communication Over Time

Vocabulary

Pony Express a mail service in which riders carried mail on horseback

invention something that is made for the first time

Morse code a way of signaling in which dots and dashes stand for letters

broadcast to send out information

Mail by Horseback

In 1775 Benjamin Franklin was in charge of the postal service, or mail. Mail sent within a city arrived pretty quickly. If mail was sent far away, it could take weeks. In the 1800s mail was sent by horseback or wagon train. Many people had moved to the West. It was hard for them to communicate with friends and family in the East.

Mail by Pony Express

In the 1800s people did not always get their mail. Sometimes robbers attacked mail wagons. Weather also caused problems. In 1860 a group of people found a way to deliver mail faster and more safely. They set up the **Pony Express.** It delivered mail to the West. Mail carriers rode horses 75 miles per day. The Pony Express cut mail delivery time in half. Then the Transcontinental Railroad was built. The postal service then sent mail across country on the train. The Transcontinental Railroad put an end to the Pony Express.

The Telegraph and Telephone

In 1837 Samuel Morse invented a machine that could send and receive messages. The machine sent signals through a thin wire. Morse called his **invention** the telegraph. An invention is something that is made for the first time. In 1861 a telegraph wire connected the eastern and western parts of the United States. People used the telegraph to send messages across the country in seconds. The signals on the telegraph were in **Morse code.** In Morse code, dots and dashes stand for letters. In 1876 Alexander Graham Bell invented the telephone. Like the telegraph, the telephone used wires. Now, people in different places could talk to each other easily.

Radio and Television

In 1896 Guglielmo Marconi found a way for voices to travel over long distances with no wires. His invention was the radio. People got information from the radio. In 1908 A. A. Campbell Swinton built a television. Words and pictures could be **broadcast,** or sent out. At first, the pictures were black and white. Now they are in color. Communication has changed even more in the past 20 years. Some telephones no longer need wires. Satellites and cables send hundreds of television channels. The Internet lets messages arrive in seconds.

Name ______________________ Date ____________ **Lesson 2 Review**

Use with pages 250–255.

Lesson 2: Review

1. **Cause and Effect** Look at the effect. Fill in the cause in the box.

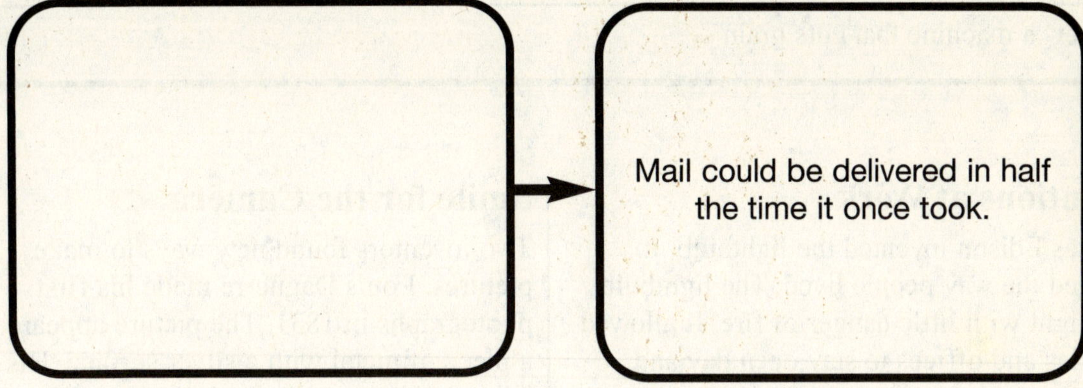

2. Why was the Pony Express set up in 1860?

____

____

____

3. How did Samuel Morse and Alexander Graham Bell change the way people communicated?

____

____

____

4. Why was radio such an important invention?

____

____

____

5. **Critical Thinking:** ***Draw Conclusions*** Why is it important to be able to communicate easily?

____

____

____

Name ____________________ Date ____________

Lesson 3 Summary

Use with pages 258–263.

Lesson 3: Inventions Over Time

Vocabulary

reaper a machine that cuts grain

Inventions at Work

Thomas Edison invented the lightbulb. It changed the way people lived. The lightbulb gave light with little danger of fire. It allowed factories and offices to stay open day and night. Lewis Latimer was an African American inventor. He worked with Thomas Edison and Alexander Graham Bell. Latimer invented many of the parts in lightbulbs and lamps that we use today. His work helped bring electric light to New York City, Philadelphia, and other cities.

Inventions in Farming

In the 1700s and 1800s, many people worked on farms. The work was hard. Harvesting was difficult. A person would walk though the field carrying a sharp blade with a long handle. The person would swing the blade to cut the grain. In 1831 Cyrus Hall McCormick invented the **reaper,** a machine that cuts grain. The reaper made harvesting crops easier.

Smile for the Camera

Two inventors found new ways to make pictures. Louis Daguerre made his first photographs in 1831. The picture appeared on a piece of metal with a silver surface. His invention led to today's photography. In 1888 George Eastman made a simple camera. He put everything a person needed to take a picture into a box.

The Information Age

In the last 20 years, inventors have changed the way people work and play. Compact discs, DVD players, CD players, cell phones, and tiny pocket computers are used every day.

Name ____________________ Date ____________

Use with pages 258–263.

Lesson 3: Review

1. **Cause and Effect** For each cause, fill in the effect in the correct box.

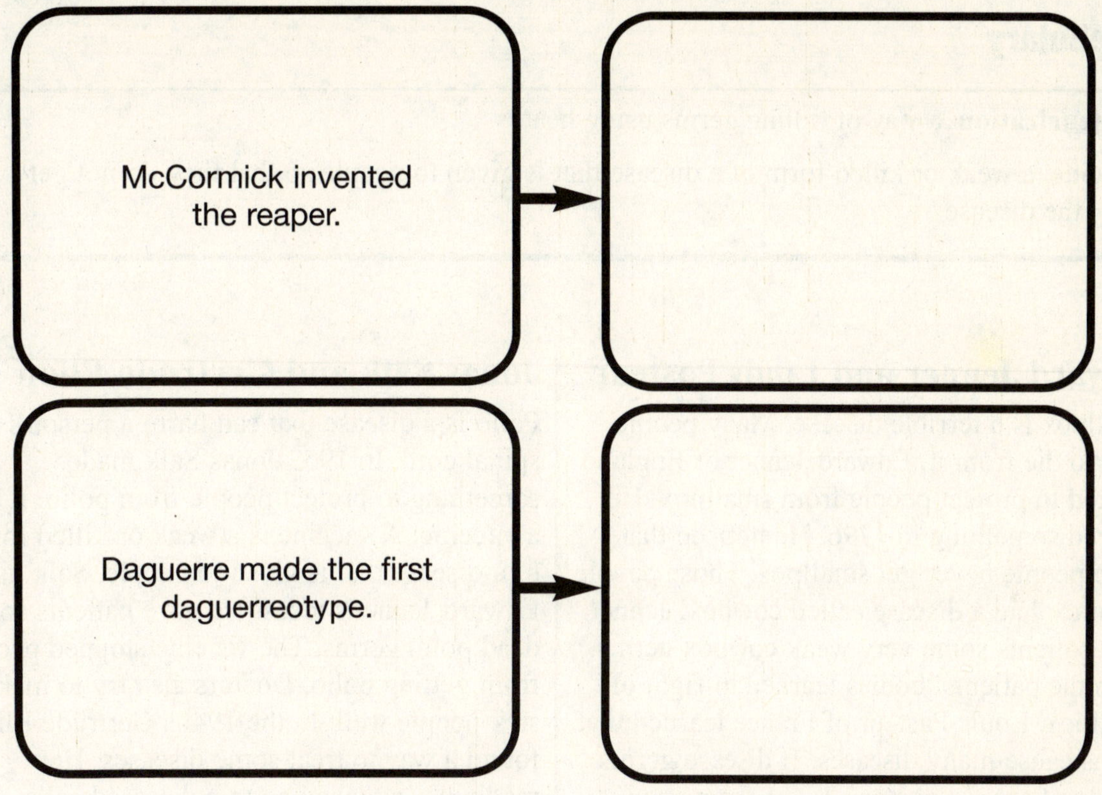

2. How did Lewis Latimer help New York City and Philadelphia?

____

____

3. How did farmers harvest crops before McCormick invented the reaper?

____

____

4. What current inventions were made possible by the inventions of Daguerre and Eastman?

____

____

5. **Critical Thinking: *Evaluate*** What computer inventions do you use every day? Which do you think is the most important? Why?

____

____

Name ______________________ Date __________ **Lesson 4 Summary**

Use with pages 266–269.

Lesson 4: Medicine Improves Over Time

Vocabulary

pasteurization a way of killing germs using heat

vaccine a weak or killed form of a disease that is given to people so that they do not get the disease

Edward Jenner and Louis Pasteur

Smallpox is a terrible disease. Many people used to die from it. Edward Jenner of England worked to protect people from smallpox. He noticed something in 1796. He noticed that some people never got smallpox. Those people had once had a disease called cowpox. Jenner gave patients some very weak cowpox germs. Then the patients' bodies learned to fight off smallpox. Louis Pasteur of France learned that germs cause many diseases. If disease germs could not enter a person's body, the person would not get the disease. Pasteur came up with a way to kill certain germs in milk. He heated the milk. We call this process **pasteurization.** This made milk safe to drink.

Jonas Salk and Gertrude Elion

Polio is a disease that can harm a person's spinal cord. In 1952 Jonas Salk made something to protect people from polio. It was a **vaccine.** A vaccine is a weak or killed form of a disease that is given to people. Salk used Edward Jenner's ideas. He gave patients some dead polio germs. The vaccine stopped people from getting polio. Doctors also try to make sick people well. In the 1940s Gertrude Elion found a way to treat some diseases. Her medicines attacked certain diseased cells. They did not harm healthy cells. These medicines saved many lives. Elion won the Nobel Prize for her work. Today medicines save many lives. Many diseases are nearly gone. People are living longer, healthier lives.

Name ______________________ Date ____________ **Lesson 4 Review**

Use with pages 266–269.

Lesson 4: Review

1. **Cause and Effect** For each cause, fill in the effect in the correct box.

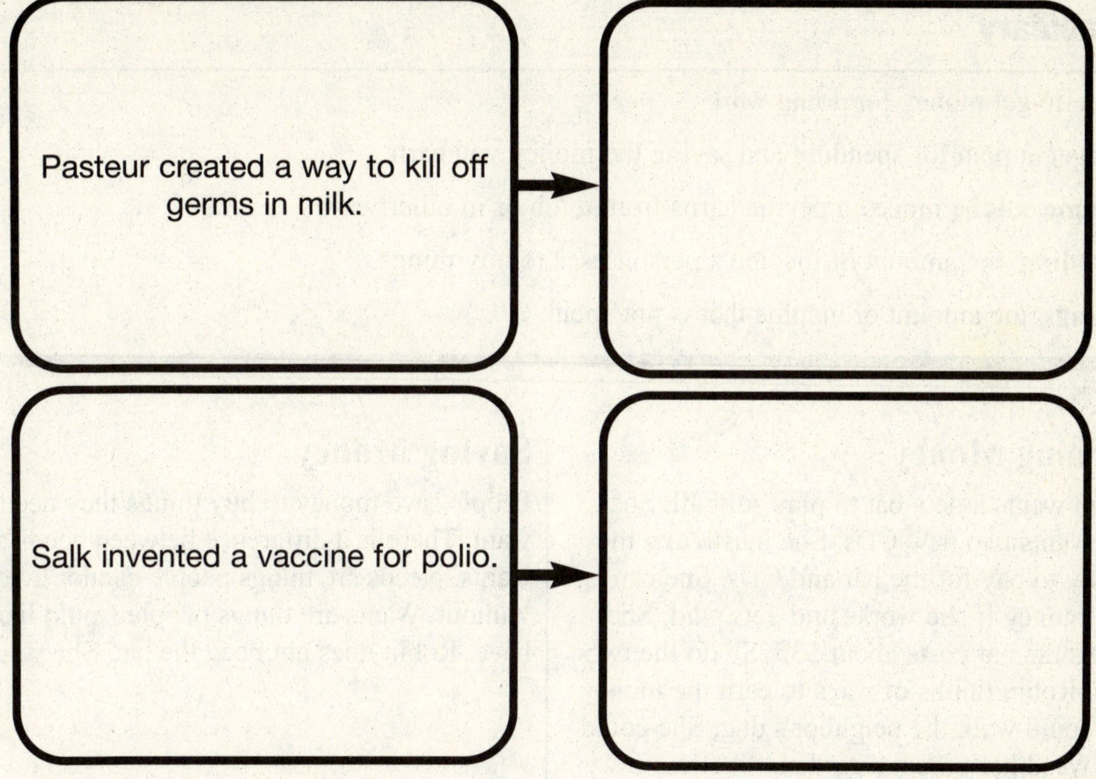

2. Describe the most important step in the process of pasteurization.

____

____

3. How is polio prevented?

____

____

4. What prize did Gertrude Elion earn for her work?

____

____

5. **Critical Thinking: *Draw Conclusions*** How did Edward Jenner figure out how to prevent smallpox?

____

____

Name ______________________ Date ____________ **Lesson 1 Summary**

Use with pages 290–295.

Lesson 1: Earning, Spending, and Saving

Vocabulary

earn to get money for doing work

budget a plan for spending and saving the money you earn

income all the money a person earns from a job or in other ways

spending the amount of income a person uses to buy things

savings the amount of income that is not spent

Earning Money

Robin wants a new bat to play softball. She also wants two new CDs. She must **earn** the money to pay for the bat and CDs. She can earn money if she works and gets paid. She knows the bat costs about $35. So do the two CDs. Robin thinks of ways to earn the money. She could walk the neighbor's dog. She could also weed her parents' garden.

Keeping Track of Money

Next, Robin makes a **budget** to help her buy the bat. A budget is a plan that shows **income, spending,** and **savings.** Robin's income is the money she makes from her jobs and allowance. Her income is $6 a week. Robin buys a snack for $1 once a week. Her spending is $1 a week. The money that she has left over is her savings. Her savings is $5 a week. Robin must save for seven weeks to get $35.

Saving Money

People save money to buy things they need and want. There is a difference between needs and wants. Needs are things people cannot live without. Wants are things people would like to have. Robin does not need the bat. She wants it.

Name ______________________ Date ____________ **Lesson 1 Review**

Use with pages 290–295.

Lesson 1: Review

1. **Sequence** Sequence some of the steps Robin used to save money.

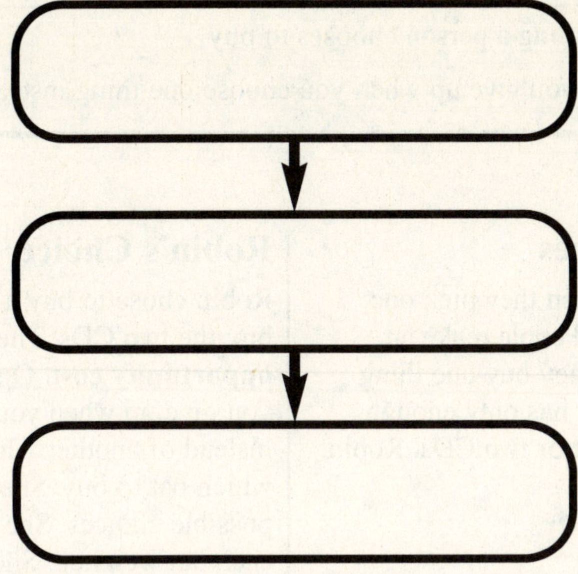

2. What are some things Robin can do each week to earn money?

____

____

3. How are savings and income different?

____

____

4. What are some examples of needs and wants?

____

____

5. **Critical Thinking: *Draw Conclusions*** What are some ways that Robin could save more money?

____

____

Name ________________ Date ____________ **Lesson 2 Summary**

Use with pages 300–303.

Lesson 2: Choosing Wisely

Vocabulary

economic choice something a person chooses to buy

opportunity cost what you give up when you choose one thing instead of another

People Make Choices

People make a choice when they pick one thing instead of another. People make an **economic choice** when they buy one thing instead of another. Robin has only enough money to buy either a bat or two CDs. Robin must make a choice.

Robin's Choice

Robin chose to buy a bat. She decided not to buy the two CDs. The two CDs were Robin's **opportunity cost.** Opportunity cost is what you give up when you choose one thing instead of another. Then Robin had to decide which bat to buy. She used a chart to show her possible choices. She thought about how much each bat weighed. She also thought about how long each bat will last. The chart helped show Robin what was important to her. Then she chose a bat to buy.

Name ______________________ Date __________

Use with pages 300–303.

Lesson 2: Review

1. **Main Idea and Details** List the choices Robin must make as she chooses a bat.

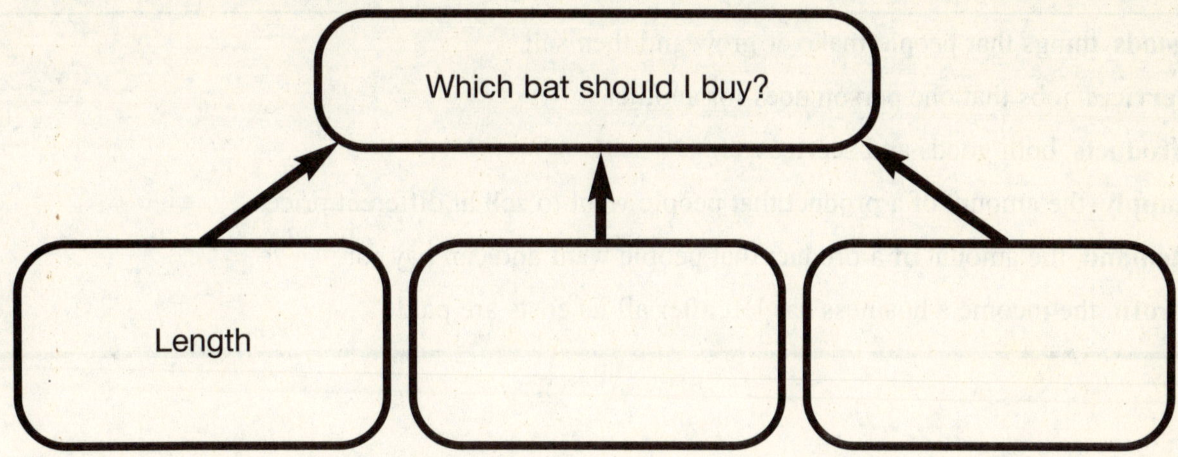

2. Identify two examples of economic choices you have made. Tell what you picked and what you gave up.

____

____

____

3. What is opportunity cost? Give an example.

____

____

____

4. How did Robin's list help her make a choice?

____

____

____

5. **Critical Thinking: *Sequence*** What steps did Robin follow as she made an economic choice to buy a bat?

____

____

____

Name ____________________ Date ____________ **Lesson 3 Summary**

Use with pages 306–311.

Lesson 3: A Community Business

Vocabulary

goods things that people make or grow and then sell

services jobs that one person does for another

products both goods and services

supply the amount of a product that people want to sell at different prices

demand the amount of a product that people want and can pay for

profit the income a business has left after all its costs are paid

Goods and Services

Most communities have large businesses and small businesses. All businesses offer goods, services, or both. **Goods** are things people make or grow and then sell. Softball bats and vegetables are goods. **Services** are jobs that one person does for another. People who fix cars offer a service. **Products** are both goods and services.

The Amount of a Product

Supply and demand can change the price of a product. **Supply** is the amount of a product that people want to sell. If supply goes up, prices usually go down. If a store has too many bats, the owner may lower the price of the bats. **Demand** is the amount of a product that people want and can pay for. If demand goes down, prices often go down. If few people want to buy bats, the store owner may lower the price of the bats.

Getting Ahead

Businesses try to make a profit. A **profit** is the income a business has left over after all its costs are paid. Costs are things that a business spends money on. A business makes a profit only when it can sell a product for more than it costs to provide it. For example, owners of sporting goods stores try to buy bats from bat makers at the lowest possible price. The store owners make a profit by selling the bats for more money than they paid for the bats. Businesses can do things to increase, or raise, their profit. One thing businesses can do is to sell a product at a higher price. Businesses also can try to keep costs down.

Name ____________________ Date ______________ **Lesson 3 Review**

Use with pages 306–311.

Lesson 3: Review

1. **Cause and Effect** Describe the different ways that prices of goods and services can change.

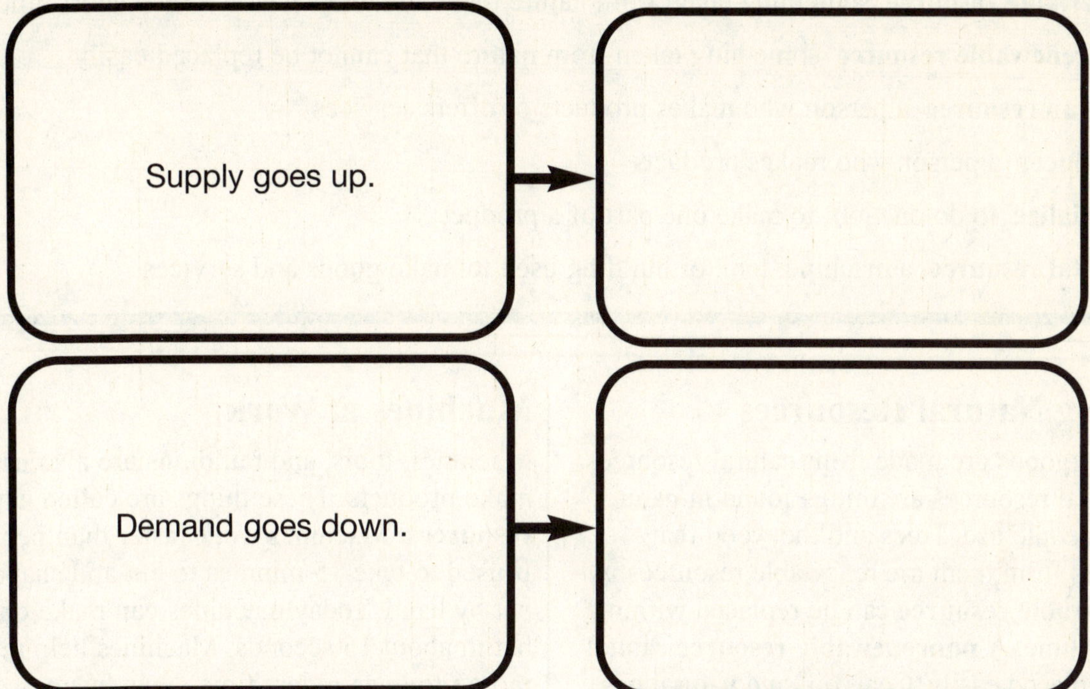

2. What are some examples of businesses that provide goods or services?

____

____

3. Would you expect the price of a valentine to be higher or lower after Valentine's Day? Why?

____

____

4. How can a business increase its profit?

____

____

5. **Critical Thinking: *Make Inferences*** If many farmers have a lot of tomatoes to sell, would you expect the price to be higher or lower? Why?

____

____

Name ______________________ Date ____________

Lesson 1 Summary

Use with pages 318–323.

Lesson 1: Using Resources

Vocabulary

renewable resource something taken from nature that can be replaced within a short time

nonrenewable resource something taken from nature that cannot be replaced easily

human resource a person who makes products or offers services

producer a person who makes products

specialize to do one job; to make one part of a product

capital resource a machine, tool, or building used to make goods and services

Using Natural Resources

Many goods are made from natural resources. Natural resources are things found in nature that people use. Trees and the wood that comes from them are renewable resources. A **renewable resource** can be replaced within a short time. A **nonrenewable resource** cannot be replaced easily. Coal, oil, and natural gas are nonrenewable resources. Inside factories, people and machines change renewable and nonrenewable resources into products. Workers in a softball bat factory make a piece of wood into a bat.

People at Work

People work to change resources into goods. People who make products are called **human resources** or **producers.** Many of these people work in factories. Today factory workers mostly use machines to make products. Factory workers often **specialize** in one job. That means that a worker makes only one part of a product. Many specialized workers might help to make one product.

Machines at Work

Machines, tools, and buildings are also used to make products. These things are called **capital resources.** Machines work faster than people. It used to take 15 minutes to cut and shape a bat by hand. Today machines can make one bat in about 15 seconds. Machines help make more products in less time. Now businesses can sell more bats at lower prices. This helps businesses make more money.

Lesson 1: Review

1. **Sequence** Sequence the steps needed to make a softball bat.

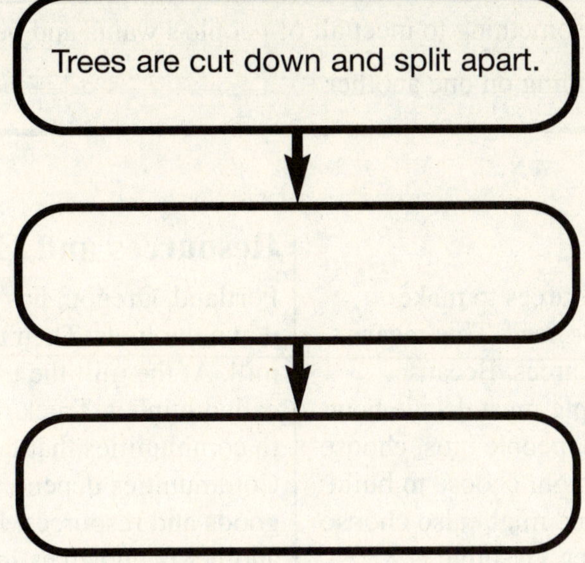

2. How is a renewable resource different from a nonrenewable resource?

____

____

3. How do specialized workers help make goods?

____

____

4. How have machines changed the amount of time needed to cut and shape one bat?

____

____

5. **Critical Thinking: *Cause and Effect*** How can machines help a company make greater profits?

____

____

Name ______________________ Date ____________ **Lesson 2 Summary**

Use with pages 328–333.

Lesson 2: Depending on Others

Vocabulary

scarcity not enough of something to meet all of people's wants and needs

interdependence depending on one another

Too Few Resources

There are not enough resources to make everything people want or need. This means there is a **scarcity** of resources. Because resources are scarce, people must decide how to use them. For example, people must choose how to use wood. They might choose to build houses out of wood. People might also choose to use wood to make paper. Gasoline is another scarce resource. In 1941 many men were fighting in World War II. Because of this, male baseball players were scarce. To meet the demand for baseball, a women's league was formed in 1943. It was called the All-American Girls Professional Baseball League. Many people enjoyed women's baseball.

Resources and Goods

Portland, Oregon, has many trees. People cut down the trees. Then they take the trees to a mill. At the mill the trees are made into boards called lumber. Truck drivers bring the lumber to communities that do not have many trees. Communities depend on one another for goods and resources. Depending on one another is known as **interdependence.**

People Helping People

Land is another scarce resource. Communities must choose how they want to use their land. Communities need money in order to build on land. When money is scarce, people in a community depend on one another for help. Some people give money. Others offer goods and services. People in communities work together and share resources.

Name ______________________ Date ____________

Use with pages 328–333.

Lesson 2: Review

1. **Sequence** Sequence the path wood takes from forests near Portland to Phoenix.

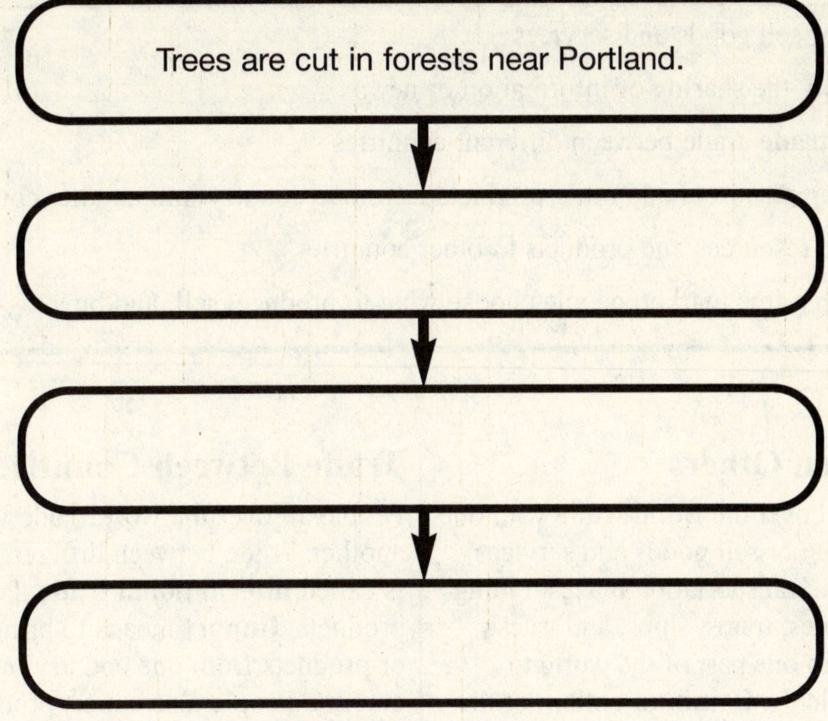

2. What are some scarce resources that people use?

____

____

3. How does wood get from the community where it is produced to the community where it is used?

____

____

4. How does scarcity cause people to depend on each other for goods and services?

____

____

5. **Critical Thinking: *Cause and Effect*** How did World War II lead to the formation of the All-American Girls Professional Baseball League?

____

____

Use with pages 334–339.

Lesson 3: A World of Trade

Vocabulary

trade to buy or sell goods and services

communication the sharing of information or news

international trade trade between different countries

import to bring resources and other products from one country into another country

export to send resources and products to other countries

free market in a free market, people choose what to produce, sell, and buy

Depending on Others

Communities all over the world **trade** with one another. They buy or sell goods and services from each other. Transportation makes trading possible. Airplanes, trains, ships, and trucks move goods from one part of the world to another very quickly. **Communication,** or the sharing of information, also helps countries trade with one another. A worker in a grocery store can use a phone or a computer to order more products.

Trade Then and Now

People traded with one another long ago. People in one place usually made only a few kinds of goods. They would trade their goods with people from another place. For example, people in ancient Greece traded with people in Egypt. Greeks made pottery. They traded pottery for goods they needed, such as wheat. Greeks used wheat to make bread. People in ancient Rome also traded with people in Egypt. Romans traded crops for silk cloth. They used the cloth to make clothing. Today people usually trade goods and services for money. One person uses money to buy a product from another. People trade with each other because trading is helpful to both of them.

Trade Between Countries

People all over the world trade with one another. Trade between different countries is called **international trade.** People import products. **Import** means to bring resources or products from one country into another country. People also export products. **Export** means to send products to other countries.

Free Markets

The United States has a **free market.** In a free market, people can decide what they want to make. They also can choose what they want to buy. Farmers may choose which vegetables to grow. People then can choose which vegetables to buy. Some countries do not have a free market. Their governments decide what people can buy and sell.

Use with pages 334–339.

Lesson 3: Review

1. **Compare and Contrast** Compare and contrast trade long ago with trade now.

Compare/Alike	Contrast/Different

2. How have modern transportation and communication changed trade?

____

____

3. What is the reason people choose to trade?

____

____

4. How did people in ancient Greece and Rome use the goods for which they traded?

____

____

5. **Critical Thinking: *Fact and Opinion*** Which of the following are statements of fact, and which are statements of opinion?
   a. World trade has made the world a better place.
   b. The United States has a free market.
   c. In a free market, people and companies decide what is bought and sold.

____

____

Name ______________________ Date ____________ **Lesson 1 Summary**

Use with pages 358–361.

Lesson 1: Governments in the Past

Vocabulary

direct democracy a government that is run by the people who live under it

republic a government in which citizens elect other people to speak for them

Ancient Greece

People long ago formed communities for the same reasons we do today. They wanted a safe place to live, work, and play. They also wanted fair laws. Citizens made laws in ancient Athens, a city in Greece. Citizens are official members of a community or nation. The government in Athens was called a **direct democracy.** In a direct democracy, citizens run the government. In the United States today, our government is a **republic.** In a republic, citizens elect people to speak for them. These people are called representatives. In 1215 King John of England signed a paper. The paper was called the Magna Carta. It said that the king had to follow the law. He also had to ask citizens before he made decisions.

Mayflower Compact

In 1620 colonists from England came to Plymouth, Massachusetts. They sailed on a ship called the *Mayflower*. The colonists left England so that they could practice their religion the way they wanted. Their leaders wrote a plan of government to make laws for the community. The plan was called the Mayflower Compact. The Mayflower Compact said that the colonists would make laws for their community. Everyone in the community would follow the laws. This was the first time European colonists came up with a plan to make laws for themselves. The founders of the United States used the Mayflower Compact as an example to follow later.

Name ______________________ Date ____________ **Lesson 1 Review**

Use with pages 358–361.

Lesson 1: Review

1. **Summarize** Fill in details that support the lesson summary.

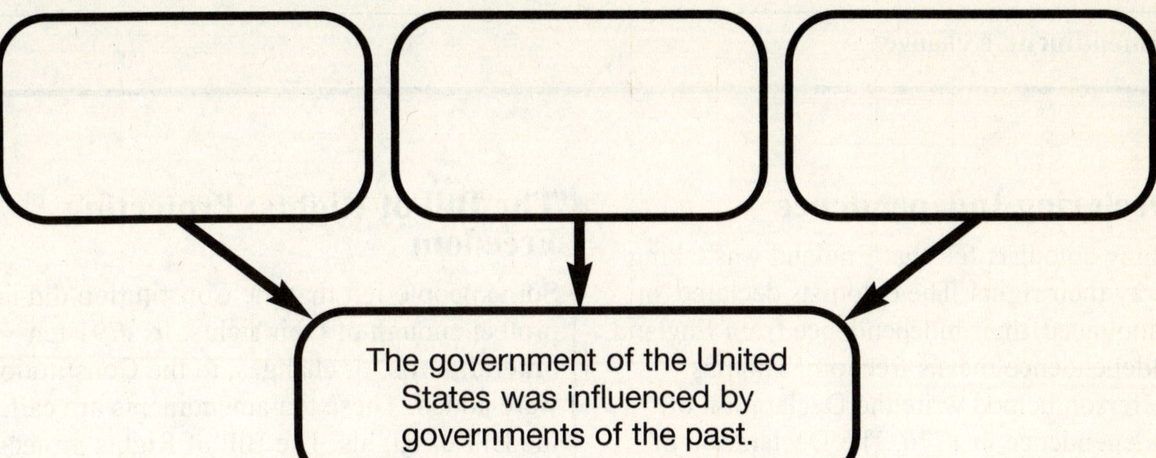

2. Why do people form communities?

____

____

____

3. Why did the English colonists create a plan of government?

____

____

____

4. Why was the Mayflower Compact an important plan?

____

____

____

5. **Critical Thinking: *Draw Conclusions*** Why do you think that the Magna Carta was an important document?

____

____

____

Name ____________________ Date ____________ **Lesson 2 Summary**

Use with pages 366–371.

Lesson 2: United States Government

Vocabulary

amendment a change

Declaring Independence

Many colonists felt that England was taking away their rights. The colonists declared, or announced, their independence from England. Independence means freedom. Thomas Jefferson helped write the Declaration of Independence in 1776. The Declaration of Independence has three parts. The first part says that people have rights. These rights are the right to life, the right to be free, and the right to try to build a happy life for themselves. The government must protect these rights. The second part lists the ways the king of England took away the colonists' rights. The third part said that the colonies were no longer part of England.

The U.S. Constitution

The U.S. Constitution was written in 1787. The U.S. Constitution is a plan for the government of the United States. Many people worked to write this plan. George Washington was the leader of the group who wrote it. Benjamin Franklin and James Madison also helped write the Constitution. The Constitution gave the people, not a king, the right to rule.

The Bill of Rights: Protecting Freedom

Some people felt that the Constitution did not protect enough of their rights. In 1791 ten **amendments,** or changes, to the Constitution were added. These ten amendments are called the Bill of Rights. The Bill of Rights protects some rights of the people. Some of these rights are freedom of speech, freedom of religion, and the right to gather together. African Americans sometimes were treated differently than other Americans. Rosa Parks tried to change this in the 1950s. Other African Americans joined her work to protect their rights. Laws were finally passed to protect all people's rights. Thurgood Marshall was the first African American judge on the United States Supreme Court. He worked to make sure that all people's rights were protected.

Name ____________________ Date __________ **Lesson 2 Review**

Use with pages 366–371.

Lesson 2: Review

1. **Summarize** Fill in details to complete the lesson summary.

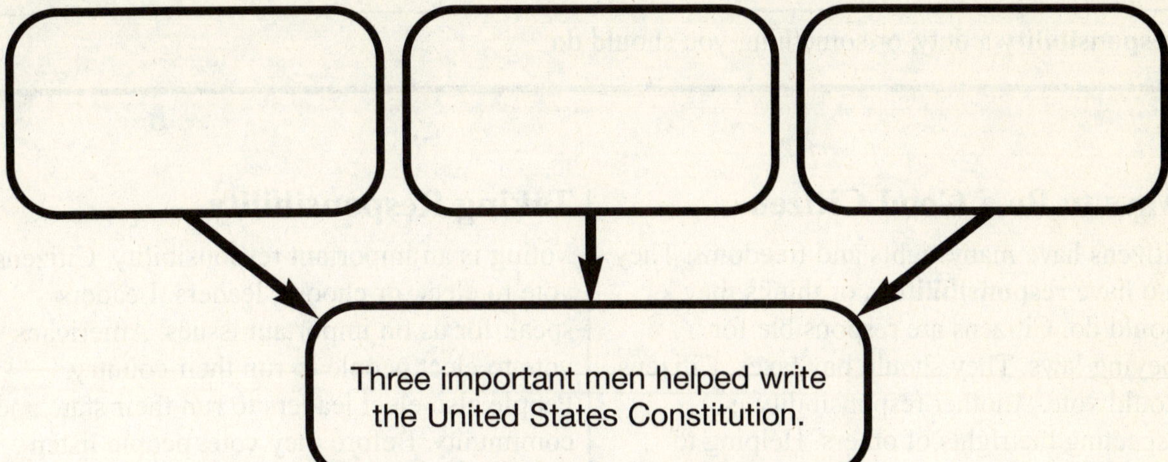

2. What three rights does the Declaration of Independence say that people have?

____

____

____

3. Why was the Bill of Rights added to the Constitution?

____

____

____

4. How did Rosa Parks's community change because of her actions?

____

____

____

5. **Critical Thinking: *Compare and Contrast*** How are the Declaration of Independence and the Bill of Rights alike and different?

____

____

____

Name ______________________ Date ____________ **Lesson 3 Summary**

Use with pages 376–379.

Lesson 3: Being a Good Citizen

Vocabulary

responsibility a duty, or something you should do

Ways to Be a Good Citizen

Citizens have many rights and freedoms. They also have **responsibilities,** or things they should do. Citizens are responsible for obeying laws. They should pay taxes. Citizens should vote. Another responsibility is respecting the rights of others. Helping to make the community a better place is also a responsibility.

Taking Responsibility

Voting is an important responsibility. Citizens vote to elect, or choose, leaders. Leaders speak for us on important issues. Americans vote to elect people to run their country. People also elect leaders to run their state and community. Before they vote, people listen to the leaders who want to be elected. Next, they decide who they think would do the best job. Finally, they vote. Working to make the community better is another important responsibility. People can make their community a better place by volunteering to help others. When people volunteer, they are not paid. They help others because they want to. People might volunteer to help people who are hungry or need clothing.

Name ____________________ Date __________ **Lesson 3 Review**

Use with pages 376–379.

Lesson 3: Review

1. **Summarize** Fill in the details to complete the summary of this lesson.

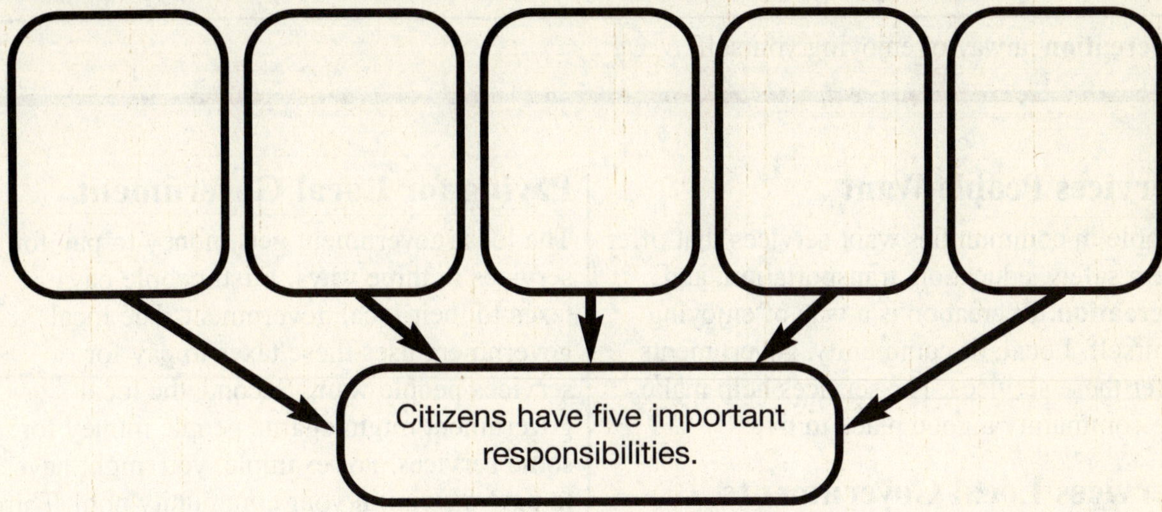

2. What is a responsibility?

3. Who speaks for the people of the United States on important issues?

4. What is one way to help improve your community?

5. **Critical Thinking: *Sequence*** What are three steps in voting for leaders?

Name ______________________ Date __________ **Lesson 1 Summary**

Use with pages 384–387.

Lesson 1: Community Services

Vocabulary

recreation a way of enjoying yourself

Services People Want

People in communities want services that offer them safety, education, transportation, and **recreation.** Recreation is a way of enjoying yourself. Local, or community, governments offer these services. The services help make the community a good place to live.

Services Local Governments Provide

Police and fire departments are services that offer people safety. They protect people. Schools are services that give people an education. People also can read books at libraries. Recreation is also important to people. Many communities have parks where people can play sports. Some communities have swimming pools. Local governments also offer transportation services. They fix and build roads. Some governments run buses and trains. It costs money for local governments to offer services. The people in your community pay for them.

Paying for Local Government

The local government gets money to pay for services in three ways. First, people pay taxes to their local government. The local government uses these taxes to pay for services people want. Second, the local government might charge people money for some services. For example, you might have to pay to swim in your community pool. Third, the local government gets money from the state and national governments.

Name ______________________ Date ____________ **Lesson 1 Review**

Use with pages 384–387.

Lesson 1: Review

1. **Summarize** Fill in details that support the lesson summary.

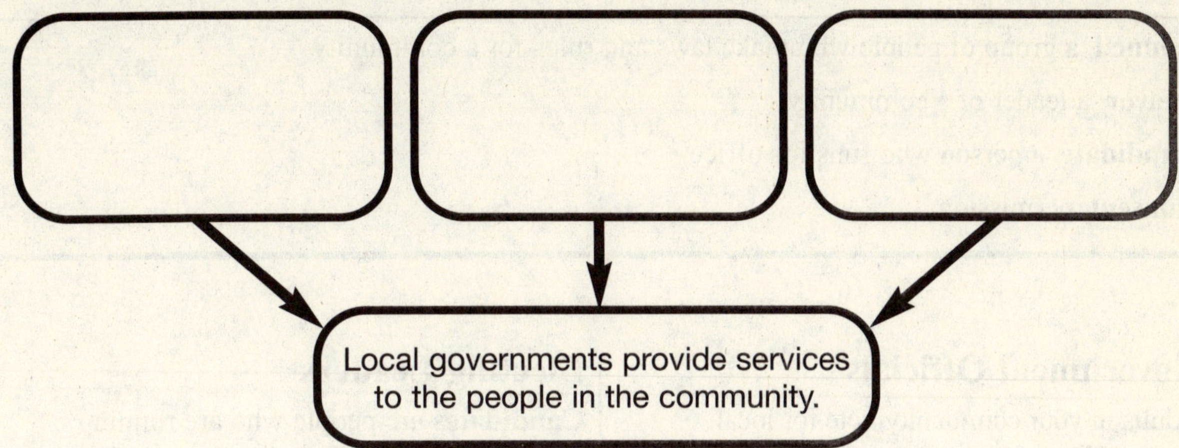

Local governments provide services to the people in the community.

2. Why do local governments provide services the people want?

____

____

____

3. What services help meet a community's need for safety and security?

____

____

____

4. Name one way that local governments get money for the services that they provide.

____

____

____

5. **Critical Thinking: *Summarize*** Identify the four types of services usually provided by local governments.

____

____

____

Name ______________________ Date ____________ **Lesson 2 Summary**

Use with pages 390–395.

Lesson 2: Community Leaders

Vocabulary

council a group of people who make laws and rules for a community

mayor a leader of a community

candidate a person who runs for office

consent permission

Government Officials

Adults in your community vote for local leaders. They elect, or choose, a town or city **council.** A council is a group of people who make laws for a community. Adults may also elect a **mayor.** The mayor leads the community. Sometimes the council chooses the mayor. The mayor and the council run the local government. They choose people to do certain jobs, such as the police chief. The park district board makes most decisions about parks and recreation activities. The citizens usually elect the members of the park district board. The school board makes rules for the community's schools. The citizens elect the members of the school board. The superintendent of schools carries out rules made by the school board. The school board usually picks the superintendent.

Electing Leaders

Candidates are people who are running for office. Candidates talk to people in the community. Candidates explain how they will help the community. The people listen. Next, they compare what different candidates have said. Finally, people vote for the person they think will do the best job.

Consent of the People

People want their leaders to make and carry out laws. People give their **consent,** or permission, to leaders to do this. People agree to follow the laws. If leaders do not do a good job, people will not vote for them again. The leaders will no longer have the power to speak for the people.

Name ______________________ Date ____________ **Lesson 2 Review**

Use with pages 390–395.

Lesson 2: Review

1. **Summarize** Fill in a sentence to summarize this lesson.

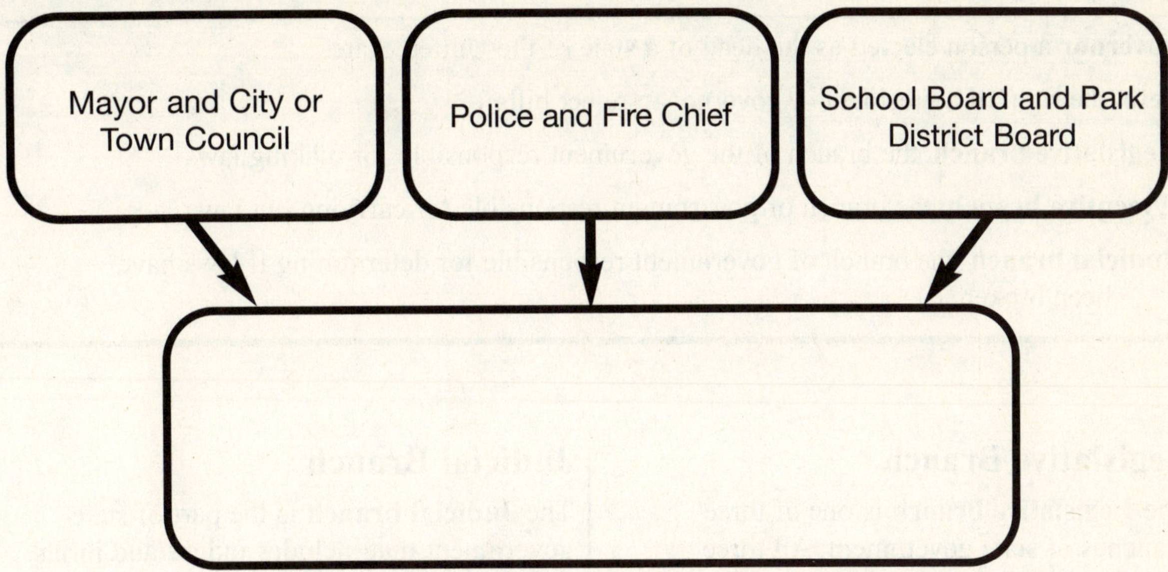

2. Identify six local officials and explain how they are chosen.

____

____

3. What happens if a leader does not do a good job?

____

____

4. Whose job is it to carry out the rules made by the school board?

____

____

5. **Critical Thinking: *Compare and Contrast*** How is government as described in this lesson the same or different from your local government?

____

____

Name ______________________ Date __________ **Lesson 3 Summary**

Use with pages 398–401.

Lesson 3: State Government

Vocabulary

governor a person elected as the head of a state of the United States

veto the right of a president or governor to reject bills

Legislative branch the branch of the government responsible for making laws

Executive branch the branch of government responsible for carrying out laws

Judicial branch the branch of government responsible for determining if laws have been broken

Legislative Branch

The **Legislative branch** is one of three branches of state government. All three branches are part of the lawmaking process. When a law begins, it is called a bill. It is someone's idea. The bill must be approved by the state Legislature before it can become a law. In most states, the two groups in the state Legislature that vote on bills are called the House of Representatives and the Senate.

Executive Branch

After the Legislative branch has approved a bill, the bill goes to the **Executive branch.** The head of the Executive branch is the **governor.** The governor might approve the bill and sign it. Then it becomes a law. The governor might disagree with the bill and **veto** it. If the governor vetoes the bill, the Legislative branch might vote on it again. If the Legislative branch approves the bill at this time, it can become a law. The Executive branch is also in charge of enforcing laws. Each state has police officers to make sure people follow state laws.

Judicial Branch

The **Judicial branch** is the part of state government that includes judges and juries. Judges and juries decide when laws have been broken. They work in places called courts. The highest court in each state is the Supreme Court.

Name ______________________ Date __________ **Lesson 3 Review**

Use with pages 398–401.

Lesson 3: Review

1. **Summarize** Fill in the three branches of state government.

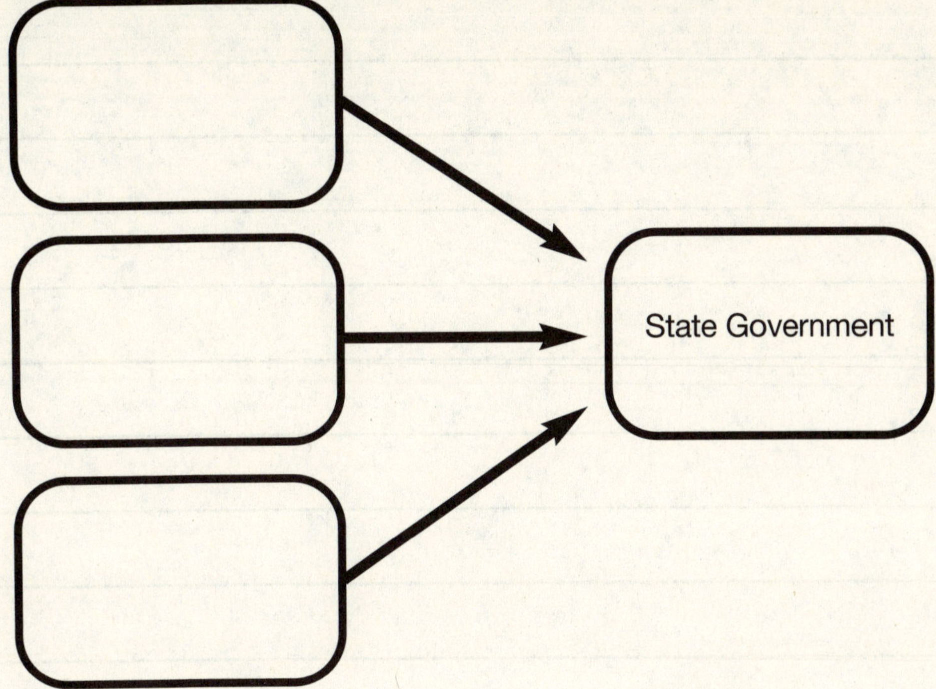

2. Which branch of government includes courts?

____

____

3. Where are bills approved before they become laws?

____

____

4. Who can veto a bill?

____

____

5. **Critical Thinking: *Sequence*** Describe the steps a bill takes to become a law.

____

____

NOTES

NOTES

NOTES

NOTES

NOTES

NOTES

NOTES

NOTES

NOTES

NOTES

NOTES

NOTES

NOTES

NOTES

NOTES